Cunningham and Other Pigs I Have Known

Cunningham and Other Pigs I Have Known

Emory Jones

Cunningham and Other Pigs I Have Known

Published by EMORY JONES LLC

ISBN: 978-1-7361034-0-1 - Hardcover
ISBN: 978-1-7361034-1-8 - Paperback
eISBN: 978-1-7361034-2-5 - mobi
eISBN: 978-1-7361034-3-2 – ePub   010421

For more information, visit our website at www.emoryjones.com.

Illustrations and cover design by Jim Powell
Legal Review by William M. House

Dedication

To my wife, Judy—thanks for holding my hand, laughing at my jokes, being my best friend and most trusted advisor.

Another special—and huge—thank you goes to the Future Farmers of America (FFA) organization.

Both the author and the illustrator are former Georgia FFA members. They credit the FFA for having made a tremendous and positive impact on their lives.

And, hey, this may be the only funny pig book ever written and illustrated by two former FFA state officers who won the Star Greenhand award.

We can't prove it, but we're pretty sure that's right.

"No man should be allowed to be president who does not understand hogs."

Harry S. Truman
33rd President of the United States

Contents

Pigs are some of the cleverest animals on the planet.
In fact, scientists who study such things say they're smarter
than dogs. Pigs have even been known to
use tools, although nothing as complicated as a
band saw. Take that, Fido!

Why I like pigs—bless their achy bacon hearts

As you can probably tell from the title, this book is about pigs I have known, both professionally and personally. Or, sometimes, only in my imagination.

And, to misquote the always late Will Rogers, I never met a pig I didn't like.

I have no idea why I developed such support for swine. It might even be genetic. But, for some reason, I did. And the sentiment kicked in early.

Perhaps it was because I grew up on a farm, and there were always pigs around.

I remember, as a tot, totting to the barn and back, sporting my little straw hat, as Granddaddy and I went to feed the pigs, milk the cows and gather the eggs. Early on, the pigs became my favorite.

The cows were nice enough, but not the pick of the litter in any self-respecting animal house. The truth is that cattle aren't very bright—even those black and white ones that work in advertising.

And—while I may get an egg tossed in my face for saying this—chickens are just plain silly. Not only do they peck you, but they'll use fowl language while doing it.

I get a kick out of horses, but a donkey will almost always make an ass of him or herself at some point, which is off-putting.

So, of all the animals down at that old barn, the pigs were the most fun to hang out with. It wasn't just the mud, either; we were just closer on an intellectual level.

As a child, my all-time favorite bedtime story was *The Two Little Pigs*. Granddaddy couldn't afford the entire book, but he did what he could, bless his heart.

During high school, I showed FFA pigs at various local fairs. I don't recall winning many ribbons, but we had fun.

After graduation, I got myself an Agricultural Journalism Degree from the University of Georgia, and that opened the gate to a lot of hog farms. It was like being a veterinarian, only without having to take chemistry or get your hands dirty.

My big break came when I was lucky enough to be the first correspondent on the scene for a superfecundation event that happened on a hog farm just south of Ionia, Iowa.

Superfecundation is hard to explain, even with an Agricultural Journalism Degree in your hip pocket.

In layman's terms, it means some sow with no moral compass has newborn pigs by one litter daddy and then, three weeks later, gives birth to a second set of babies from a different litter daddy. At least that's how the veterinarian explained it to me while scrubbing his hands.

I wasn't surprised. You could tell that sow was a floozy just by looking at her.

I guess I feel the same way about pigs as Winston Churchill did, when he once said, "It is my observation that dogs look up to us, cats look down on us, but pigs treat us as equals. Give me a pig anytime."

Now, I realize not everybody understands my and Sir Winston's fondness for swine.

But all we are saying is give pigs a chance.

Not only are they smart, but they're also the only animal on earth that can convert vegetables into bacon.

Pigs are loyal, too. And they hardly ever chase cars. They also won't squeal on you when you come stumbling home late at night the way a dog will.

Anyway, this book is about pigs. It includes the many adventures of one particularly notorious pet pig I call Cunningham. I hope you'll come to love ole Cunningham as much as I do, although I don't think my wife, Judy, ever will.

I hear the younger generation doesn't care all that much about pigs.

But they will—when they're older. The swine pendulum always swings.

And please understand that there is nothing new about people keeping pigs as pets.

In fact, some historians now believe humans may have first housebroken hogs as far back as the Saus-Age.

Pigs hate hot weather. This is why you'll never find one vacationing in Arizona. You see, it's almost impossible for pigs to sweat. Mud baths not only cool them off, but act as a sunscreen and insect repellant, too. Pretty smart if you ask me.

A brief history of pigs

Fossilized farm records indicate pigs have been around for millions of years in one form or another. At least that's what I've heard.

The earliest pigs showed up in either the jungles of Asia or the swamps of Europe, depending on who you ask.

But it was the Chinese who first domesticated pigs.

Hieroglyphic records show that a newly elected emperor made a key plank in his national platform be to have his country win the global pig race. He demanded Chinese scientists put a farm-raised pig on his table by the end of the decade, which, according to my calendar, would have been 6,160 BC.

"But Your Excellency, we don't know what domesticated means," said the spokesman for the Chinese scientists. Of course, he said that in Chinese.

"Look it up," the Emperor wisely replied, also in Chinese.

Then, seeing the blank look on the spokesman's face, the Emperor sighed. "Just grab a few pigs from the woods, build a bamboo pen and put them in it. If we don't hurry, those Europeans will beat us to it."

The subjects accepted the challenge, formed a think tank, and made it happen a year ahead of schedule in 6,151 BC.

A few BC's later, sweet and sour pork had replaced sweet and sour horse on menus all across Asia.

Over the centuries, pigs became so crucial to the human race that when Señor Hernando de Soto—who later had a car named after him—and his bunch landed in Florida in 1530-something, they had several hogs on board the boat.

While historians differ on the exact number, I personally think having any hogs on board the boat at all was most likely due to a mistake on the manifest. I mean, what sailor ever loaded up a ship and then thought, "Let's see. We've got gunpowder, cannons, cornmeal, extra underwear for the men… that should about do it. No, wait. We'll probably need a few hogs, too."

I don't think so.

Instead, since de Soto was noted for his poor handwriting, it was more likely he'd ordered several hogsheads of rum instead. Some rookie explorer probably read it wrong, and they were already at sea before anybody noticed the mistake.

That poor rookie likely spent a few days in the brig after the boss ordered up his first rum and ginger.

De Soto also brought the first horses to Florida, but since this book is about pigs, I'll just say this about that: History records that while de Soto's men were unloading the boat, he turned to some Juan on the aft deck and shouted, "¿Los caballos siguen en el barco?"

Roughly translated, that means, "Are the horses still on the boat?"

Juan, who spoke two languages, yelled back, "No, Señor. THEY'RE OFF!"

And thus, the first horse race in America happened just outside what is now known as Sarasota. At least that's what I've heard.

There's probably lots more I could say concerning the history of pigs, but this is about all I know for certain.

If I write any more, I'll just be making it up as I go.

Breaking a pig chain

One of my early experiences with pigs involved losing my FFA pig-chain pig.

Those of you who weren't active in the Future Farmers of America like I was, may not know what a pig chain is.

If you fall into that category, don't bother looking it up because I'm about to fill you in.

Sometime after one of the world wars—I forget which—somebody at Sears and Roebuck decided that starting a series of livestock chains would be the next logical move for the company. Although this pig chain thing was more like a chain letter.

I guess management felt that since Sears already sold chain saws and chain-link fences, farm-animal chains would be a natural progression.

While I realize the Sears Foundation ran the program for other farm animals, like cows and even chickens, let's stick to pigs for this discussion. The idea was that they'd give, free of charge, five high-quality female pigs and one reasonably decent male version to FFA and 4-H clubs all across the country.

The chapters would then distribute the six hogs to six even higher-quality students the pig chain committee had deemed worthy to be entrusted with a free pig.

To be one of the selected few was quite an honor.

The six lucky recipients would then raise the fine swine. Among other things—including a monthly inspection by the pig chain committee—they also agreed to show their free pigs at the fair that fall.

Then, roughly 114 days after a conjugal visit from the male pig, a whole new set of baby pigs would start the cycle over.

The idea was brilliant, actually.

I don't think my grandmother was ever as proud of me as she was the day I told her I'd been picked to be a pig-chain pig recipient. I still get emotional thinking about it.

When it came time, the whole family piled into the car and headed to the north end of the county to pick up my pig from one of last year's graduating pig chainers.

I regret to this day nobody thought to bring a camera.

I held the wee little girl pig in my lap all the way home. Grandmother sat beside me, beaming.

My mother kept honking the car horn and pointing with pride to the back seat every time we passed one of the neighbors' houses. She was proud of me, too, bless her heart.

I put the little pig I'd already named Doodle Bug into the pen I'd so lovingly made for her down by the barn.

That next morning, I got the shock of my life. Doodle Bug had rooted a hole under the fence and escaped! I guess, sweet thing that she was, she missed her mama.

At first, I thought Grandmother was playing another one of her little tricks on me. Then I realized not even a grandmother would joke about losing a pig-chain pig.

Nobody would.

I looked everywhere, but Doodle Bug was gone. She'd disappeared faster than my wife, Judy, does when my pet pig Cunningham and I catch another rerun of *Hee Haw* on RFD-TV.

Late that afternoon, one of the neighbors stopped me on the side of the road.

"I heard you lost a pig," she said.

"How did you know?"

"It's all anybody's talking about," she answered. "You should be ashamed of yourself."

There was nothing I could say because she was right.

Then, I guess the neighbor lady felt sorry for me because she leaned out the car window and whispered, "Look. Up to now, you've always been a good kid. I saw a little pig running up the road this morning on my way to work. It was headed north. But I can't be a participant in a pig chain scandal. So, if you tell anybody I told you this, I'll deny it. I hope you understand."

She cranked the window up before I could ask more questions.

So, north I went. Finally, I came upon the largest pig farm in our part of the county. The owner was there, looking out over roughly three hundred little pigs, all the same size and color as Doodle Bug.

"I lost my pig-chain pig," I mumbled.

"I heard," he replied.

"How?"

"On the morning farm report."

"Have you seen her?" I asked, facing my shame head-on.

"Son, I've got three hundred pigs that look exactly like your Doodle Bug. How would I know?"

"You wouldn't," I admitted.

Then he said, almost kindly, "If you can pick Doodle Bug out of the herd, you can take her on home with you. I mean, if you can catch her."

Then he added, "And if you think it's the right thing to do."

It wasn't, of course. Doodle Bug had found a home among her own kind. I couldn't take that away from her.

It took a while, but Grandmother finally started letting me sit at the table again.

But she never really got over that whole pig chain scandal. In fact, she was the only family member who didn't show up to see me get my Agricultural Journalism Degree from the University of Georgia.

But I think that was mostly because Sears and Roebuck refused to send us their catalog anymore.

Life, liberty and
the pursuit of sunburned pigs

Even though I'd once misplaced my pig-chain pig, my grandmother loaned me five dollars to acquire another one the following year. That may not sound like enough money to buy a pig, but remember, you could get a *good* one for as little as twelve dollars in those days.

I named this one Doodle Bug and a Half. And, while I didn't lose this Doodle Bug, I did let her get sunburned one time.

You see, it was a tradition for us FFA members to take several girl pigs, known as gilts, and a few boy pigs, known as boy pigs—at least the lucky ones—to the Georgia Mountain Fair in Hiawassee.

And on this particular trip, those pigs got so sunburned on the way over, they were just shy of being premature bacon bits.

We'd always spend the days before the show getting them ready by washing, waxing (that's an entirely different thing with pigs) and generally trimming things up for the fair.

Our agriculture teacher, Mr. Fitzpatrick, would then help us load the hogs on the straw-covered floor of the blue, flat-bed truck with high sideboards and giant FFA decals on both sides. Then we'd head out.

That fall, we had one hog on board named Groucho. Another was Piggy Sue. And one especially creative FFA member called his two pigs Oscar and Meyer.

Another was aptly named Slim. Nobody had great hopes for Slim, but since the little fellow didn't take up all that much room, we brought him along anyway.

It was a blue-sky day, and those of us riding in the back (nobody considered that dangerous then) kept the pigs on their sides in the straw. The ride over was so pleasant, we didn't notice the sun beating down on our Yorkshires.

By the time we got to the fairgrounds, all our hogs except Slim, who'd hunkered down between Oscar and Meyer, had a pink glow to them.

Knowing red pigs—that were supposed to be white—would not sit well with the judges, Mr. Fitzpatrick drove the truck to town for talcum powder. We always shook a bit on the pigs before a show anyway, just to freshen things up a bit.

But this time, although we'd doused them with enough powder to cover most of the redness, we couldn't apply enough to conceal the soreness.

As with people, there are several stages of pig sunburnness, and while unloading them, we discovered our hogs had reached the stage that makes them ornery. In fact—just like with people—a sunburned pig is seriously ill-tempered.

The old FFA manual we all carried back then didn't mention what to do in case your pig became sunburned. I guess that just never came up in those pre-pig-show planning meetings.

As I recall, the handbook simply stated, "While in the ring, move slowly and calmly. Keep your pig fifteen feet from the judge and maintain as much eye contact with that individual as possible."

That all sounded fine on paper. But until you've tapped a sunburned hog on his ham hock with a show stick, the idea of all heck breaking loose is just a theory.

Doodle Bug and a Half squealed like she'd just landed the starring role in *Charlotte's Web*. Groucho, flouting the fifteen-foot rule, charged the judge, who was suddenly the last person on earth anybody wanted to make eye contact with.

Moving slowly and calmly went out the window, too.

Except for Slim—who won the "fastest of show" ribbon—we didn't bring home any awards that year. But, as Mr. Fitzpatrick pointed out, the manual also says, "No matter what happens, there's always another show, another judge and another year."

Mr. Fitzpatrick's job was to teach us about agriculture. I guess no one ever told him he could stop there because he taught us about life, too.

And that sometimes, usually when you least expect it, you're going to wind up with a sunburned pig on your hands.

And when you do, you can throw the darn manual right out the window.

Frank the pig

North Dakota is flat compared to my native North Georgia, but it's an amazing place, nonetheless.

For example, did you know the geographical center of North America is in northern North Dakota? Well, it is, and they even have an obelisk marking the exact spot. I remember that so well because it's the first time I ever heard anybody use the word obelisk.

Also, North Dakota—at the time of this writing at least—is the only united state that's never had an earthquake. I'm not an earthquakeologist, but my theory on why North Dakota has never had an earthquake is that the earth up there is frozen so hard it can't quake.

Anyway, I'll always remember North Dakota as the place I met Frank the pig. It happened while I was interviewing a wheat farmer on assignment for the *Gluten Free Press*.

They say the most common prayer offered up in North Dakota is to ask the Good Lord to please let summer fall on a weekend. I'm not sure when summer fell that year, but it did not go down while I was around because it was COLD!

I guess the farmer felt sorry for me and my southern-type blood because he walked us to the house for a cup of warm coffee. Warm is about as hot as coffee can get up there.

So, there we sat, with the farmer talking about his wheat, and me taking numerous notes with a frozen number two lead pencil, when I happened to glance into the man's living room.

Having won the FFA Star Greenhand award (I cite this merely to establish credentials), I know a pig when I see one. Even if the swine I saw was stretched on a couch, covered with an afghan, its head on a pillow.

No doubt about it—there was a pig in a blanket on this man's settee.

Now, I was raised to mind my own business, but I couldn't keep chatting about wheat when there was a sow on the sofa. (Frank was actually a boy pig, but I wanted to work in that "sow on the sofa" line, so thanks for bearing with me.)

Still, I hesitated to say anything, because you never know where things stand in a situation like this. I mean, did the farmer even know the pig was there? Would he be furious when he found out?

Someone slipping a pig into your parlor could be the end result of a nasty divorce.

Who knows?

Finally, I had to ask. So, I interrupted his discussion of planting depth variations by variety to inquire, "Sir, are you aware there's a hog in your home?"

Turns out, he knew all about the situation. "Oh sure," he said. "That's Frank. Would you like to meet him?"

Because of the differences in our accents, I wasn't sure if he said, "meet him" or "eat him," but I figured "yes" would be the polite response either way. So, we went into the living room, which smelled fine (come on—I know you were wondering).

The farmer bent over the sleeping hog and whispered, "Frankeeeee, we've got companeeeee. Wake up and meet your new friend, Frankeeeee."

Frank arranged himself on the couch and offered me a hoof in friendship while the farmer filled me in. A few years back, they'd bought a baby potbellied pig for a pet. By the time they discovered Frank's DNA wasn't calibrated for petite, he had literally grown on them.

The farmer explained his pig was not only housebroken but smart, too. "Here," he said. "Let me show you."

Then he told the pig, "Frank, go outside and fetch the newspaper."

Frank said no. I mean, he shook his head and grunted what I'm fairly sure was pig for, "ARE YOU CRAZY?? IT'S COLD OUT THERE! SUMMER HAPPENED THREE WEEKENDS AGO!!"

The farmer opened the door. I can't repeat what Frank grunted next, but he was walking toward the mailbox when he grunted it.

Then Frank—squealing with every frozen step he took— sprinted down the driveway, grabbed the newspaper in this mouth and, still shrieking shrilly, raced back to the house to drop the paper at the farmer's feet.

It was an impressive thing. I mean for a pig. If it had been a dog, I wouldn't have thought twice about it.

But here's the kicker: do you remember Mr. Charles Kuralt, the man who used to travel the country interviewing interesting people? Well, early one Sunday morning, a year or so later, I heard the TV announcer say, "Stay tuned as Charles Kuralt interviews Frank, North Dakota's only piano-playing pig!"

And there was my ole buddy, hamming it up on the upright!

I know pigs are clever, ranking just behind dolphins and slightly ahead of Congress. Still, I found Frank's piano playing to be remarkable.

Not that he was all that good at it, but because not once during my visit did he ever mention being a performer.

Most pigs aren't that unassuming.

The pig is the twelfth and last symbol in the Chinese zodiac. Folks born during the Year of the Pig are said to be intelligent and creative, with a strong sense of responsibility. If you work in human resources, you might want to keep that in mind.

It's time to legalize pig racing

Looking back, taking my pet pig, Cunningham, to the horse races a while back may have been a mistake. But then again, maybe not.

At any rate, it seemed like a good idea at the time, although my wife, Judy, was bad against it. But you have to understand— that woman is opposed to any road trip involving pigs. I guess it must be a female thing because both my sisters are the same way.

Anyhow, Cunningham was so excited about going to the track, I couldn't say no to him.

The pig has racing in his blood. He won't brag about it, but as a young shoat, he once won the NASPIG Triple Crown. This means he came in first in the *Sue Wee Classic, The Running Ham Handicap* and the grueling *Bacon Crisp Steaks.*

He almost crowned even those achievements by winning the *Swine Breeders Cup*, but the track was muddy that day, and he got distracted. So did several other pigs, which allowed a long shot named Hot Dog to win by a shoulder.

Unfortunately, all those events had to be held across the state line because Georgia continues to cling to its outdated pig-racing rules which, believe it or not, still outlaw this spectacular sport within its boundaries.

I don't want to get political here, but focus groups indicate the next person who runs for governor on a pro-pig-racing platform has a ten-to-one shot of winning by three lengths.

I had read in the last issue of my *All Pork, All the Time* magazine that Kentucky was ahead of us when it came to legalizing this worthy pastime. The magazine said there had even been talk of making Churchill Downs, home of the famous Kentucky Derby, a pig track. Every other year, anyway.

So, naturally, Cunningham and I wanted to see for ourselves.

In the end, Judy agreed to come along with us as long as we drove to Louisville in separate vehicles, which, to my mind, isn't really going "with us" at all, but that's just me. Anyhow, she left in her car before I even got Cunningham's seatbelt fastened good in the truck.

And, just as I could have predicted, that woman got lost and wound up spending the entire weekend in Myrtle Beach instead of Kentucky.

It's not the first time that's happened, either.

Judy not riding in the same car with us was fine with Cunningham. He and she never can agree about what stations to listen to on the radio—she's classical, he's country.

Now, if you've ever been to that Churchill Downs horse racetrack, you know how strict they are about not letting you bring your own food inside. One time back in '09, they even confiscated two cans of Vienna sausages from my cousin Wayne—talk about harsh!

Turns out, they apply that same off-putting policy to pigs.

"Whoa there," said the gate guard, who, I guess, was trying to get some sort of horse theme banter going. "Is that a pig?"

"You bet your jockey strap it is," I said, playing along with his racy talk.

"Well, he can't come inside."

"Why not?" I asked with unbridled curiosity. "He has a ticket."

"Because he's a pig."

"You let horses in, and pigs are way smarter than horses."

When the gate guard reached for what I imagined to be a starting pistol, Cunningham sprinted toward the infield.

Since that pig sometimes gets in trouble by himself, I bolted after him, despite the gate guard's warning whistle. I might have caught Cunningham, too, if I hadn't spotted that "buy one, get one free" special they were having on mint juleps that day.

By the time I caught up with him, Cunningham had already rooted under the fence and inadvertently wandered onto the track.

His timing couldn't have been worse because those starting gates for the first race were just swinging open.

When I yelled at the pig to run, he heard the field coming behind him and lit a shuck for the finish line with a dozen horses bearing down on him hard. The pace was fast.

The crowd and I roared together as Cunningham finished first by a snout. The next day's *Louisville Ledger* called it the most thrilling race since a jockey named Pat Night raced *Sotally Tober* around the track backward in 1967.

By the time I elbowed my way to the winner's circle, Cunningham, not understanding the subtle differences between horse and pig racing, had eaten half the roses the stewards had so graciously hung around his neck.

It didn't matter much, though, because, despite what that magazine said, Kentucky may even be less forward-thinking about pig racing than Georgia is.

Instead of seeing Cunningham's win as historic, two of the racing stewards took the half-eaten roses away from him and ordered us off the premises.

They didn't even take our picture.

We got the last laugh, though. On the way out, Cunningham ran over to one of the horses lying down to sun himself between races and planted a little sign which read, "Help! I've fallen, and I can't giddyup!"

We laughed about that all the way home.

March 1ˢᵗ is National Pig Day. Really. According to that occasion's founders, National Pig Day exists "to accord the pig its rightful, though generally unrecognized, place as one of man's most intellectual and domesticated animals." Hey, I'm as surprised about this as you are.

Seeing eye to eye with a pig

Except for my wife, Judy, folks who meet my pet pig, Cunningham, nearly always talk about how helpful he is. For a pig, I mean.

And, I must admit, when it comes to lending a hand (in his case a hoof), that big boy always brings home the bacon and then some. He even had me assist him in forming a local chapter of "Pigs Helping People," but, sadly, as so many startups started by swine do, it went belly-up.

Anyway, I wasn't surprised when he trotted up a few days ago toting a little brochure from the *Sardis Special Seeing-Eye School for Pigs*. It took me a while to find Sardis on a map, but I finally did.

Becoming a seeing-eye pig has long been one of Cunningham's dreams. However, a recent fact-finding trip to a nearby gaming club had inadvertently left me short of funds.

Still, it's tough to put a pig off. So, instead of admitting I was broke, I told Cunningham Sardis didn't have a feed store. At the same time, I suggested a learn-it-at-home course would be a much better option.

I also explained that housing costs in Sardis—as I hear they are all over Asia Minor—are high. Especially for pigs.

Surprisingly, Judy offered to help out with Cunningham's living expenses if I'd let him go. I guess she wanted the pig to have the "on campus" experience, but I don't think he's ready to leave home yet. Plus, he's horrible with money.

Luckily, the pig agreed. So, we went on the innerweb and learned how to make a homemade, pig-sized, seeing-eye harness from one of Judy's umbrellas, an old tire, and some hog-wire. That innerweb is something else, I tell you what.

Cunningham wanted to commence training right away, so we started by having him guide me around the yard blindfolded. That didn't go well—too many trees. But everything went a lot smoother once the meds they gave me at the emergency room kicked in.

After that, I decided to give Cunningham a "real world" experience someplace other than in our yard. My cousin, Wayne, sees well enough, but he's been blind drunk so often, I thought he'd be the perfect person to put Cunningham through his paces. It would be sort of like a final exam.

So, we blindsided Wayne at his muffler repair shop and headed for town.

Everything went well at first. Wayne, as I had asked him to do, kept his eyes closed while Cunningham led him around the courthouse parking lot like a pro.

Then, regrettably, something no one could have predicted happened: the wind shifted.

As I explained to the deputy later, that's when Cunningham picked up the scent of a peppermint pig pellet truck headed north toward The Old Sautee Tea Room and Pig Food Store east of Helen.

Quicker than you can say *greased pig*, Cunningham took out after that truck. I guess he was hoping a bag of pig pellets might inadvertently fall off when the driver made that sharp right turn north of town. After all, it *had* happened before. Twice.

Wayne, eyes still shut, had no choice but to go along, since he'd somehow caught his mood ring on the umbrella part of the harness.

I should point out here that my pig suffers from color-blindness—he gets it from his mama's side—so he didn't realize the cross-walk light was red and dragged poor ole Wayne right into the oncoming traffic.

A sea green Peterbilt, probably loaded with pig iron out of Peoria, sat waiting to make a left turn at the intersection. To humor some kids pumping their arms up and down, the driver honked his air horn.

At the same time, a pickup with Arkansas plates, pulling one of those shiny silver campers and proudly sporting an "Everything's better in Birdeye" bumper sticker, stopped behind the big green rig.

The camper door opened, and a lady wearing nothing but a pink slip, fuzzy house slippers, and a set of those extra-large Sears and Roebuck hair curlers looked out. I guess she thought they'd arrived at their campsite early.

Anyway, spooked by the air horn, Cunningham panicked and dragged Wayne right inside the camper with that lady.

There was a whole lot of shaking going on. But the woman's husband apparently didn't notice because, when the light changed, he hit the gas hard enough to knock a fence post loose.

Cunningham, Wayne, and the lady in the pink slip kept bouncing around inside until they got about halfway around the square. At this point, she swept both of them out the door with her broom.

I don't know who screamed the loudest, Wayne or the pig, but several people incorrectly reported an air-raid siren had gone off.

Cunningham and my cousin raced around the courthouse the wrong way twice before the pig refocused on that pellet truck. You can't blame him because, as good as those things smell to people, we can only imagine what they must do to a pig.

At any rate, he was soon racing up the highway with Wayne doing his darndest to keep up. If his mood ring hadn't still been caught up in that harness, I don't think he could have.

My cousin could have helped himself by not hollering so, but I guess it did smart some when he banged his head against that bank sign that flashes the temperature.

By the time I caught up, Cunningham was pulling Wayne around in a circle in the Huddle House parking lot. My cousin was holding on with one hand while fishing in his pocket for one of those piggy treats he keeps there for his own pet pig, Jerry Lee.

That puzzled me.

"Why are you giving Cunningham a piggy treat," I asked? "He liked to have killed you."

"Piggy treat my petunias!" said Wayne. "I'm trying to get him to hold still long enough for me to kick his little pork butt!"

I couldn't help but laugh because Cunningham still had one of the camper lady's hair-curlers dangling from his ear.

Pig on parade

I'm surprised my pet pig, Cunningham, hasn't got the big head.

Actually, he sorta has, but I can't really blame him for that.

Because, shortly after landing the off-stage role of Joe the Rooster in a play I wrote called *Cheever*, Cunningham was asked to participate in a parade through downtown Helen.

In the old days—back when landlines roamed the earth—Cunningham would answer the phone by nudging it off the hook and grunting into the receiver. But now that "Mr. Pig Shot," as my wife, Judy, affectionately calls him, has his own cellular telephone, he wanted her to start taking his calls for him.

She respectfully declined due to time constraints. Anyhow, that's my job now.

So, when the pig's phone rang late one afternoon, I answered it for him. "Cunningham's residence," I said, using the executive tone I used to use back in my advertising agency days.

"Is he available?" asked the caller.

"For what?" I inquired suspiciously, switching back to my regular voice. All those crank calls inviting Cunningham over for a barbecue just aren't funny anymore.

"To ride in a float during the annual parade kicking off the Oktoberfest season," he said.

Suddenly, I recognized the man's voice. This was the President of the Parade Committee.

"Oh. You mean TAP-KOO?" I asked, suddenly interested. Cunningham's ears perked up, too.

"What did you just say?" the man asked.

President of the Parade Committee or not, he had to be "from off" if he didn't know TAP-KOO is short for what we locals call The Annual Parade Kicking Off Oktoberfest. But I let it ride.

"I'll check Cunningham's calendar," I replied.

Then I really did check the pig's calendar. Not many people can say they've ever done that, but I'm proud to be one of the few who can.

All Cunningham had down for that date was a quick trip to take some acorns to the home for blind hogs, so I asked him if he'd agree to be in the parade, too.

"Grunt," he snorted.

"I doubt they'll agree to that," I said.

Cunningham gave me the ole pig eye, so I went back to the phone.

"He'll only do it if he can be the Grand Marshal."

"What?"

"The Grand Marshal. Of the parade. TAP-KOO always has one."

The President of the Parade Committee thought it over for a minute. Then he said, "Fine with me. Your pig can call himself the Grand Ole Opry for all I care."

Cunningham held out for two ears of corn and even got them to throw in a post-parade mud bath. He's been good at haggling ever since he read that *Art of The Squeal* book.

When the big day arrived, he tried to act all nonchalant about it, but I could tell he was thrilled. Being Grand Marshal of TAP-KOO is a big deal; I don't care who you are.

When we pulled into the staging area, I noticed a crowd gathering down by the river. Cunningham naturally assumed it was a group of fans who'd heard his play performance. So, he began rooting around for the number two lead pencil he uses to make his autograph mark.

Once he located it, we walked down to the river only to find the President of the Parade Committee showing off his buddy's prize pet rooster, Sir Randolph Scott, to a few onlookers.

It was then that I noticed someone had, for some reason, wired a chicken coop to the back of the lead parade tractor.

"Why is there a chicken coop wired to the back of the lead parade tractor?" I asked, halfway dreading the answer.

"It's for this prize rooster, Sir Randolph Scott, to ride in. He's the Grand Marshal of this year's TAP-KOO, you know."

"Since when?"

"Since now."

"But you promised my pet pig he could be Grand Marshal," I said politely, yet firmly. "He's been looking forward to it all week."

"Oh, yeah. Sorry about that. But I was overruled."

He didn't seem sorry to me, so I asked, "By who?" I'm pretty sure I should have said "whom," but I just wasn't thinking straight at that point.

"By one of Helen's founding fathers. I forget which."

"Do you have any paperwork confirming that?" I asked.

At that point, he waved a letter typed on Helen notepaper in front of my face. Even worse, his letter had been signed by three different founding fathers and two county commissioners.

Sir Randolph Scott crowed just to rub it in. Unfortunately, the driver of the lead tractor inadvertently took his crowing as the signal to start the parade.

In what I still believe to be a fit of excessive exuberance, the person driving the World War II model ambulance sounded its antique siren at the same time.

The prize rooster thought a giant chicken hawk was swooping down. Naturally, as chickens always do, he panicked. Then he flapped his wings, flew to the Chattahoochee and landed on one of those little pink innertube rafts that always seem to be floating by on that part of the river.

To my surprise, the woman on the raft was the very same lady from Birdeye, Arkansas, who we practically met in Cleveland when Cunningham was rehearsing for that seeing-eye pig exam.

I almost didn't recognize her without her extra-large hair curlers, but I was glad to see she was having a good time on their trip.

The President of the Parade Committee, bless his heart, sprinted after his buddy's prize rooster and dived headfirst into the river to save him.

Cunningham's natural chase instinct kicked in, or maybe he just wanted to help save the chicken's neck, too, because that's the kind of pig he is. Either way, he jumped right in the river with them.

Unfortunately, the pig's bulk created a wave large enough to capsize the little pink innertube raft like it had hit an iceburg in the North Atlantic.

This dumped the Arkansas lady into the water alongside the President of the Parade Committee.

I guess Sir Randolph Scott's feathers didn't get wet enough to keep him from flying over and landing on a nearby picnic table.

That stupid chicken made a lovely family from Lilburn, who were eating lunch there, spill a half-gallon of sweet tea. Fortunately, it looked like they were about through eating, anyway.

As I told the deputy later, the last I saw of the President of the Parade Committee and that lady from Arkansas, they were both using Cunningham like another pink raft. Then they all floated out of sight just north of the Nora Mill waterwheel.

Fortunately, I was able to grab a seat on the last float out and represent the pig in that year's TAP-KOO parade.

I refused to represent the chicken, though.

Cunningham was pretty bummed when he got home. He not only missed that year's TAP-KOO, but he didn't get his free mud bath either.

The pig stayed sulled up over that for a month.

But I had a grand time throwing candy and apples at the kids.

Especially the whiney ones.

A pig named Big Bill holds the record for being the biggest pig in modern times. Back in 1933, this porker weighed in at 2,552 pounds. Big Bill stood five feet tall at the shoulder. When Bill died, his owner had him mounted and charged people a dime a look.

Rock City road trip

Ever since I gave my pet pig Cunningham his own pet rock for his birthday—he immediately named him Hudson—he's wanted that little nugget to see Rock City.

In case you've never been, Rock City is the appropriately named spot up near Chattanooga, Tennessee, where they have the biggest bunch of rocks you'll find east of the Mississippi. I imagine there are more impressive sites in the Rocky Mountains, but I'm just guessing.

Cunningham first saw a big plug for that place, painted on top of a barn just outside Bell Buckle, on our way home from the horse races. I must admit, the sign was well done. I mean, for barn art, anyhow.

Giving Cunningham his own pet was a rock-solid idea because it's taught him responsibility. Not a lot, mind you, because he's a pig. But, since rocks don't have to be fed, watered or neutered, caring for one isn't all that hard.

Still, Cunningham takes his rock for walks and, for more formal occasions, dresses him up in one of my wife, Judy's, old socks.

He especially likes to take his rock, Hudson, on field trips. We have selfies of us and his pet in front of famous places like the hard rock candy store in Rock Spring, the Rockmart city limits sign and, of course, Stone Mountain.

Cunningham is saving up for a trip to Boulder, but to be honest, pigs are not good with money, so it may take him a while.

Now, I understand people will be debating the merits and demerits of companion rocks for years to come. But, while my wife refuses to let me purchase one for myself, even she admits a pet rock is perfect for a pig.

Oh sure, rocks can be hard to handle in the wild, but once domesticated and with the rough edges knocked off, you'll never have a more solid friend in a fight.

My wife still doesn't get it, but I know why Cunningham wanted to take his pet rock to Rock City. You see, Hudson is a country rock, and I'm sure the pig thought it would do his pebble good to see how city rocks live.

Plus, I'm pretty sure Cunningham wanted to see the place for himself as much as anything.

When the big day came, I packed a couple of ham sandwiches, and with Hudson and Cunningham both safely strapped in the truck's front seat, we headed north.

I let them listen to rock music the entire trip.

After we parked in the Rock City parking lot, I looked around for a rock to scotch the wheel but, ironically, couldn't find one.

At the gate, I asked the guard, "How much is a ticket?"

"Is that a pig?" he asked back, pointing at Cunningham.

"It is," I said proudly. "Why? Do pigs get a special rate?"

"What's in his mouth?" he asked, not answering either of my questions.

"That's his pet rock, Hudson. Cunningham wants to take a picture of all three of us with those seven states your brochure mentions in the background," I said politely.

Then, sensing this conversation might be rolling downhill, I added, "Of course, we'd love to have you in the picture, too. I mean, if it's okay with your supervisor."

Evidently, it wasn't, because he replied a little more testily than I thought necessary to a paying customer. "We don't allow pigs in Rock City. Never have. Never will."

"It doesn't say so in the brochure," I answered respectfully. I wish now I'd mentioned that nothing had been painted concerning pigs on that barn outside Bell Buckle, either. Instead, I just stated the obvious by pointing out, "It's not like pigs are going to break much of anything here."

I thought I had him there, but I guess I didn't because he took a step forward and pointed toward the parking lot. Then he blew his whistle for good measure.

Sensing trouble, Cunningham charged like General Custer at his next-to-last stand. I had no choice but to follow. And—as the brochure promised—we ran past incredible rock formations, magical caves, and breathtaking views.

I know it was only in my head, but at one point, I thought I spotted a gnome.

The brochure also says you can experience Rock City at your own pace. Unfortunately, my pace was a dead run tracking a squealing pig carrying a pet rock while being chased by Rock City security.

Cunningham gained ground on the swinging bridge, although I nearly had him when he stopped to see those seven states. Then he took off again and slid through Fat Man's Squeeze like a greased pig.

I don't think I ever would have caught him if he hadn't piled into that stack of red and black birdhouses outside the gift shop.

At that point, I casually bought a chunk of fudge and we headed on back to the truck.

All in all, it was a fun day, although we never did get that picture Cunningham wanted.

Pigs have relatively poor eyesight compared to dogs or cats. But what a sense of smell! Their snouts are about 2,000 times more sensitive than ours. This makes me wonder what people must smell like to a hog. It can't be pretty.

Rock City rescue mission

As you may recall, especially if you've been reading these stories in order, I recently took my pet pig, Cunningham, to Rock City. He wanted his pet rock, Hudson, to see the place and maybe learn more about his little stone's ancestry.

We've already traced the little nugget's lineage back to the Stone Age, but for a rock, that's not all that far.

Unfortunately, our visit didn't go as well as we'd hoped, and we left the place sooner than originally scheduled.

We were almost to the state line when Cunningham sat straight up in the seat and started squealing like a guinea pig.

"What's wrong?" I asked, stopping in the middle lane so traffic could easily pass by on either side. I would have turned on the truck's emergency flashers, but the fuse for those burned out years ago.

Cunningham's problem was that he'd inadvertently left his pet rock, Hudson, back at Rock City. He must have dropped him during all the excitement when the two of them bumped into the stack of birdhouses outside the gift shop.

Emory Jones

Clearly, we had to go back. Unlike so many pet rock owners, particularly the inexperienced ones, Cunningham does not take his rock for granite.

With the help of several motorists honking their horns in encouragement, I finally got the truck across the median and headed back north on the four-lane.

I still can't get over how often folks up that way honk their car horns. They must have some sort of civic-pride plan in place to encourage that.

When Cunningham and I arrived back at Rock City, the same fellow who was all but ready to sic the dogs on us the first time, was still on duty. He must have remembered who we were because he immediately reached for the security phone again.

"Hold on," I said politely. "There's no need to call your supervisor. I'm sure he's a busy man. I mean, if he's not a woman."

That seemed to calm him some, although he still said, "I told you, we don't allow pigs in Rock City."

I started to point out again that neither their brochure nor that barn in Bell Buckle mentioned that, but I held my tongue. After all, working at Rock City is probably hard, especially if you don't have the right shoes for it.

"We just came back to pick up my pet pig's pet rock," I said. "We left him here by mistake. His name is Hudson."

"The pig's name is Hudson?"

"Of course not," I said. "Hudson would be a horrible name for a hog. My pig's name is Cunningham. Hudson is his pet rock."

The man looked puzzled, so I restated my purpose more clearly.

"We think Hudson is hiding by that stack of See Rock City birdhouses over there," I said, pointing.

"Let me see if I have this straight," he replied. "You think your pet pig's pet rock is hiding over there by those birdhouses?"

"Yes, sir. If you'll just let him trot over there and pick up his little rock, we'll be getting on back toward the house. We're from Cleveland. The one in Georgia. Not the one in Tennessee. Although, I'm sure your Cleveland is nice, too."

When it looked like the guard was about to go for his phone again, I had to think fast.

"LOOK! OVER THERE!" I shouted. "IT'S BIGFOOT COMING ACROSS THE SWINGING BRIDGE!"

He wasn't, of course. I just made that up.

But, when the guard turned to see for himself, I motioned for Cunningham to go for it while I kept the man busy looking for Bigfoot.

Cunningham isn't the fastest pig in the world—the title goes to a big barrow named Chris P. Bacon out of Iowa—raced over and grabbed Hudson in his mouth.

I probably could have kept the guard distracted even longer with that Bigfoot story. But just then, Cunningham and Hudson once again knocked over those darn birdhouses in much the same manner they did on our first visit earlier in the day.

We all raced back to the truck while the guard blew his whistle, yelling, "Bring that rock back!"

Then he tossed one of those See Rock City birdhouses in our direction. I guess he felt guilty about not letting the pig in and wanted us to have a parting gift.

Even though he threw it pretty hard, I caught it on the fly.

Still, the man kept yelling that it's against the law to take a rock from Rock City. I guess he had to keep up appearances in case his supervisor was watching

I'm fairly sure he was bluffing about it being illegal to take a rock home, though because they would have a sign up there saying so if that were the case.

Plus, I don't think you can charge a pig with much of anything. Not in Tennessee, anyway.

Anybody who thinks they can, must have rocks in their head.

We once went to war over a pig. It was a brief clash between the United States and England. It started in 1859 when an American shot and killed an English pig on an island near Washington State. In the end, though, the pig was the only casualty.

Letting your pig paint
can turn him into a ham

I've been encouraging my pet pig, Cunningham, to get out of the house more. So has my wife, Judy, but I don't think it's for the same reason.

Last winter, Cunningham spend most of his time behind the sofa, watching television. I think his disappearing behind the couch has more to do with the inbred instinct pigs have that causes them to lay low at what used to be hog-killing time, as much as anything else.

It's sort of like how you don't see any deer in the woods during hunting season.

At least, that's what I've heard.

But once spring was in the air again, the warmer weather must have finally got Cunningham's blood pumping. Because, one morning, he muted the TV before the Dr. Dolittle movie he was watching even got to the good part, waddled over and laid a moist brochure in my lap.

The pamphlet was about the art lessons they give up at the Helen Arts and Heritage Center in downtown Helen.

They call it that because the place offers arts and heritage in the center of Helen.

Anyway, I wasn't surprised Cunningham picked up that brochure somewhere because he has always intended to paint. He decorated his pigsty all by himself, and the neighbors still talk about how it looks.

Always eager to encourage the pig's artistic pursuits, I went to the center's web place and filled out the application form myself. It's harder for a pig to type than most people think.

Since the questionnaire didn't have a block for listing species, I didn't mention that Cunningham was a member of the swine family.

I think it's against the law to ask that question, anyhow.

I also left out the part about him only being three.

The day classes started, I loaded Cunningham in my truck and headed toward Helen. He wanted to ride in back, but I was afraid he'd catch a cold despite the scarf I'd found in Judy's closet and wrapped around his neck.

Plus, his little beret might have blown off.

On the way up, we picked up a hitchhiker. I think it's only right to do that if you're the one who knocked them down.

After that, we arrived at the Arts Center, where a stern-looking lady in a colorful, paint-covered apron cracked open the door before we even knocked on it.

"May I help you?" she asked, inadvertently blocking our way.

"We're here for an art lesson. In plain air if you can arrange it," I said politely. "I think that's probably best for a pig, don't you?"

"I think you mean *en plein air.*"

"Yes. That's what I just said."

Apparently, the lady was hard of hearing, so I spoke louder. "I said the pig would like to paint outside if possible! We've already filled out the application on your innerweb site!"

She stepped back a ways and looked at me funny, so I explained further. "The art lesson is for the pig. I'm just his driver!"

To fill the silence, I crossed my fingers and said even louder, "The town Burgomaster himself gave us this brochure."

That was a *tiny* bit untrue, although I did have my fingers crossed behind my back. Truth is, I didn't even know what a Burgomaster was. I was just hoping that using a big word like that might impress her.

I was beginning to wish I'd signed Cunningham up for ballet lessons instead of an art class. But, when it comes to dancing, that pig has four left feet.

The art lady wasn't the least bit impressed with my use of the Burgomaster word because she said, "I don't care if the *governor* sent you. We don't give art lessons to pigs!"

"It doesn't mention that in the brochure," I pointed out. "I admit he's only three, but in pig years, that's close to retirement age."

At this point, the lady tried to close the door. But Cunningham, feeling slightly slighted, carelessly said something he shouldn't have in that guttural voice pigs so often use at the wrong time. I'm not even going to repeat what that pig said.

I guess she understood, too, because she slammed the door, lowered the blinds, and switched off the "open" sign, pretty much all in one motion.

We must have caught her on a bad day.

Cunningham was disappointed, of course, but he had to admit, it was his own fault for swearing at the lady. I still felt terrible for him, so we stopped at the store on the way home and bought a paint-by-numbers set.

Even without any formal training, Cunningham is getting good. In fact, he's been working hard on a self-portrait he hopes to have done in time for Judy's birthday.

However, I'm afraid all this is going to his head because he's planning a spring exhibition and keeps insisting I call him Pigasso.

The story of "The Three Little Pigs" is usually told from the pigs' point of view. However, a 1989 illustrated children's book presented the whole affair from the wolf's perspective. It's called "The <u>True</u> Story of the 3 Little Pigs." It's good. Trust me.

Camping with Cunningham

I always try to take my pet pig, Cunningham, camping over the Fourth of July holiday weekend. It's as much of a tradition as the firecrackers part.

My wife, Judy, won't come with us, though. You see, while I'm a big fan of camping, Judy is an even bigger fan of *not* camping.

She sees the entire experience as giving blood, one mosquito at a time.

When I explained early in the marriage that sleeping outdoors was a tradition in my family, she explained back that it was a tradition in *everybody's* family until somebody invented the house.

Still, always supportive of my pig getting out more, Judy was nice enough to help us pack by tossing Cunningham's sleeping bag out the upstairs window. The woman has a good arm, too, because it landed right on top of the truck. In fact, it barely even made a dent.

Once Cunningham and I got everything loaded up, we decided that nice little park they put up in the downtown Cleveland area might make a good camping spot. From there, we could watch the Historical Society's fireworks display and still not get caught up in all that holiday Dairy Queen traffic.

Everybody else in town must have had the same idea because there wasn't even any place to park at the park, let alone make camp. Plus, for some reason, somebody had put up a big NO CAMPING (EXPECIALLY PIGS) sign.

Finding the employee parking lot behind the grocery store, where we'd camped the year before, had been roped off, we headed for Helen. I thought it might be quiet up that way, what with this being a holiday weekend, and all.

Turns out Helen was not only not quiet but had even more restrictive rules on pig-camping than Cleveland did. I don't want to get into it too much here, but I don't believe they even make exceptions for seeing-eye pigs.

Happily, Hortonville, a posh suburb north of Helen, has a much more enlightened view of pigs. So, Cunningham and I found a nice spot near the highway, pitched our tent, and settled in for the evening.

To properly commemorate the Fourth, I had secretly brought along a special fireworks package. I bought it when Judy wasn't looking, on our last vacation over in Fair Play, South Carolina.

In addition to several hundred regular firecrackers, the packet included a dozen above-ground spinners, nine M-80-and-one-half outfitted Green Dog Roman candle rockets, several Happy New Year sparklers and two dozen chain-fused bottle rockets.

We normally had a much larger selection, but Judy was particularly watchful that year.

I also brought along a bag of marshmallows for supper.

While I got a fire going, Cunningham got busy gathering toasting sticks. As he was dragging one of the longest branches back to camp, he inadvertently hooked the big end on the bag of fireworks and pulled them into the roaring fire, which I may have allowed to blaze just a little too high.

The result was the mother of all premature detonations.

As I told the deputy later, I had the presence of mind to calmly roll under the truck, but Cunningham was just a little shy of being scared to death. In fact, he panicked and lit a shuck toward Helen.

We finally found him floating down the river on one of those little rubber dinghies they rent out to tourists.

By the time I fished him out of the water, he was so distraught, I had to call a hambulance to transport him to the hog hospital in Homer.

Judy must have expected our camping trip to go poorly. Otherwise, why would she have phoned ahead to say if her husband came to the hog hospital with a pig, to go ahead and have him neutered.

I'm still not ready to talk about what happened next.

Neither is Cunningham.

Hibernation is not for hogs

I didn't get my pet pig, Cunningham, to the hog hospital in Homer last fall in time for his annual swine flu shot.

The pig was so worried about catching something, he decided to teach himself to hibernate and just sleep through the whole swine flu season.

I never did think this hibernation thing was a good idea, but my wife, Judy, was all for it. I don't believe she feels the pig gets enough rest anyway because she's always offering to help me put Cunningham to sleep.

But he's more comfortable when it's just me tucking him in.

Despite Judy's encouragement, I still resisted the pig's plan. First of all, can you imagine how bad a hog's breath would be after he's been asleep for two or three months? It's bad enough now.

Besides, pigs aren't natural hibernators. If they were, hog farms would shut down for the winter. No, I believe this foolishness is more about eating than sleeping.

You see, the thing that sealed the deal was when Cunningham saw a documentary about bears on the Ursidae TV channel a few days ago. Instead of giving him nightmares like the ones he has after secretly watching those wolf documentaries behind my back, he was fascinated.

He especially liked the part where the bears eat themselves silly to get fat enough to sleep through the winter—sort of like my Aunt Tiny.

So, when the next cold snap hit and Judy was on a sleepover at her mama's house, Cunningham saw his chance. He'd already started the "eating-himself-silly" part weeks earlier, so he was raring to go.

After he downed one last bucket of table scraps, I reluctantly helped him swallow two Tylenol PMs and one of his nerve pills.

Cunningham soon went to sleep behind the sofa under a pile of my old leisure suits, for what he assumed would be a long winter's nap.

Like many pigs his age, Cunningham suffers from sleep apathy. If fact, I think he could stay up all night. But this time, he was sawing logs in ten minutes.

We were both still snoozing when Judy got home the next morning and decided to do some much-needed vacuuming. And for some reason that I, to this day, still don't understand, she decided to vacuum behind the couch where Cunningham was busy hibernating.

I guess Judy wasn't expecting a pig to be back there because it startled her and Cunningham both when she vacuumed up against his little pork butt.

Judy squealed almost as loud as the pig and threw the vacuum cleaner clean across the room where it landed on the mantelpiece, knocking over our wedding picture.

Cunningham thought the alarm had gone off for spring.

Thinking he hadn't eaten for three months, the pig smacked his lips and lit out after Judy when she ran from the room. I imagine he assumed she was rushing to fix him a large, post-hibernation breakfast.

Usually, I would take charge in a situation like this, but I noticed a rerun of *Gunsmoke* starting on the TV in the bedroom, and I got distracted.

I guess when Judy hit the kitchen, her cat, Rowdy Yates, jumped on top of the pig and stayed there by sinking his claws into the poor pig's fatback.

Judy didn't shut the front door fast enough to keep the squealing Cunningham from racing outside with the attached feline howling all fifty-seven known cat noises at the same time.

The neighbors thought a tornado warning had gone off.

Most of the dogs in our area love dashing after cats *and* pigs, but seldom get to do either. So, they saw this chance to chase both of them at the same time as a once-in-a-lifetime opportunity.

I don't think Cunningham even noticed all those dogs trailing him. Because, still thinking he was starving, he headed north toward The Old Sautee Tea Room and Pig Food Store. That's the place that sells Cunningham's favorite food—peppermint pig pellets.

Their slogan used to be "A free gallon of sweet tea with every purchase," but they had to change that due to inflation.

Anyway, Cunningham headed in that direction, taking the attached cat and an undetermined number of dogs along with him.

The store's loading dock director, who raises colorful chickens for a hobby, and owns that stupid prize rooster he calls Sir Randolph Scott, testified later that even the animal control people didn't believe his report.

And, you have to admit, a story about a starving pig, ridden by a cat, while being chased by a pack of howling hounds and what was later determined to be a rabid raccoon, would be hard to swallow.

Especially from somebody who would name a rooster Sir Randolph Scott. Even a prize one.

I would have named him Colonel Sanders.

Or maybe Russell Crow. Cluck Norris is good, too

Anything but Sir Randolph Scott.

Pigs are not only loyal, but some are patriotic, too. During WWII, a pig named King Neptune helped raise $19 million in war bonds by being auctioned off over and over. When "The King" died in 1950, they gave him a military funeral with honors.

Cunningham misses the party—not on so-called guest list

My pet pig Cunningham's social skills are far superior to those of the majority of other pigs.

Dogs, too, for that matter.

He's just not a sloppy hog. I mean, as far as hogs go.

Consequently, I was somewhat taken aback at the surprising resistance to his presence at the recent retirement event held in honor of longtime local newspaper legend Mr. Billy Chism.

Cunningham has long been a faithful supporter of the retiring editor. He even took the man's side on the newspaper's controversial support of damming Dukes Creek to provide much-needed water for Dillard.

So, you can imagine our surprise when Cunningham was turned away from what many called the social event of the season.

The announcement in the paper said the entire county was invited. Naturally, we assumed that included us. My pig hadn't been this excited since his sister came in second at the hog fair in Homer.

Always looking for a good PR angle, Cunningham came up with the idea of surprising Mr. Chism by trotting up between speeches, toting a little gift apple in his mouth.

He practiced his approach all week.

When I told my wife, Judy, about the pig's plan, she jokingly suggested I give Cunningham himself to the Chisms as a present instead of just an apple.

I couldn't do that, of course. But her proposal did give me an idea: I *could* let Mr. Chism and his lovely wife, Patti, keep Cunningham over the weekend at their retirement house in Toccoa. It would be a treat for all three of them.

That pig jumped all the way to cloud nine when I told him about my idea. Besides, downtown Toccoa is where Cunningham gets his toenails done, so we could knock off two birds with one rock.

When the big day came, Cunningham wanted to ride to town in the back of my truck, but I made him sit up front. That way, we'd both still be fresh and well-groomed when we arrived. I had even splashed on a little Old Spice for the occasion.

It smelled so nice, I put some on my own face, too.

Although we got there early, the hill at the community center was already covered in cars. I spotted two mayors and a probate judge before we even got parked. Cunningham decided to wait in the truck while I went inside to set everything up for his big apple-toting entrance.

The recreation coordinator for the parks department met me at the door. When I told him about our plan to have Cunningham present his apple during the ceremony, he went all "official" on me.

"The mayor himself is presenting Mr. Chism with a nice plaque. We don't need an apple. Besides, you can't bring a pig in here."

"Why not?"

"Because."

"The newspaper said the whole county was invited."

"Not pigs," he said, crossing his arms.

In the crowd behind him, I spotted a junior county official's wife holding one of those little near-sighted cock-eyed spaniels that always look like they need glasses.

"I see a dog in there."

"No, you don't."

To avoid hurting Cunningham's feelings, I went back to the truck and told him everybody was delighted to have him there.

Then I crossed my fingers and said they had suggested a better plan might be for me to hide him in the back of the brand new Chism family vehicle. That way, he could pop up later and surprise them on the way home.

Cunningham loved it! I thought he might—that "new car" smell is one of his favorites.

So, I hung a note around his neck, explaining that he had my permission to be in their vehicle unattended and to spend a three-day weekend with them over in Toccoa.

Then I covered Cunningham with a blanket, slipping a 10-percent-off coupon for the pig toenail place underneath.

The car was parked in the shade, but I cracked the window a little anyway. I hated doing that, but the door was locked, and there was no other way to slip the coat hanger wire in. Besides, Mr. Chism isn't the type not to carry good insurance.

Once Cunningham was comfortable, I went back to hear the speeches.

When it was over, everybody came out to pile presents in the car. Cunningham got plunked on the head by a piece of pottery the Historical Society presented to Miss Patti.

He squealed a little, but everybody was so busy slapping Mr. Chism on the back, nobody noticed.

Our plan went perfectly until the happy couple drove off, waving. Instead of waiting until they got to Clarkesville as he'd planned, Cunningham was so excited he leaned across the seat to announce himself before they even left the parking lot.

Unfortunately, that caused Mr. Chism to inadvertently hit the Subaru's brakes so hard the hatchback door sprang open.

The sudden stop caused Miss Patti to holler out loud. Because of several recent and unfortunate incidents at home involving my own wife hollering out loud, Cunningham panicked.

He jumped out of the car and raced up that steep hill toward the funeral home, dragging the blanket with him. We never did find that 10-percent-off coupon.

Before I could get him out from under their new hearse, I heard Mr. Chism's tires squeal as he drove off, which was surprising since two sheriff's deputies were standing right there.

Naturally, Cunningham was disappointed, but I promised him he could spend a whole week at the Chism home soon.

Judy has suggested I go with him, but I feel like that might be imposing.

It's not nice to hurt a pig's feelings

My pet pig, Cunningham, and I recently had a brief falling out.

You see, through no fault of my own, these little pieces I write about the pig's adventures—much to my wife's surprise—won a nice award from the Georgia Press Association.

Unfortunately, the newspaper put *my* picture in the paper instead of the pig's.

I knew there would be trouble as soon as I saw it, so I tried to keep Cunningham from finding out. But between social media, TikTok and television, keeping anything from a pet pig nowadays is pert nigh impossible. I hear it's even worse with dogs.

Still, I had to try. First, I told Cunningham his computer had caught the Coronavirus and had to be quarantined for fourteen days. Then I unplugged the television and cunningly convinced him the darn thing had died.

After that, I hid the newspaper behind the Frigidaire. But all was for naught because, as any farmer will tell you, it's hard to keep much of anything from a pig if he wants it enough.

Once Cunningham found the newspaper, it didn't take him long to spot the picture of me grinning and holding that plaque. Naturally, he wanted to know what was up.

Being quick on my feet, I told him I'd won a Weight Watchers award for losing thirty pounds. Looking back, I probably should have fabricated a more feasible falsehood, but it's hard to think fast when you've got a pig staring you down, quick on your feet or not.

Skeptical, Cunningham carried the soggy paper to my wife, Judy, who was as surprised as the pig to see my picture there. You know what they say, behind every great man is a woman rolling her eyes.

Judy usually refuses to read newspapers to pigs—it's just the way she was raised—but this time, for some reason, she made an exception.

After learning the honor was about him and not me, Cunningham did what any pig would do—he ran away from home.

Usually, when my pig runs away from home, he gets hungry pretty quick and comes right back. Either that, or he hangs out at The Old Sautee Tea Room and Pig Food Store, doing stunts in return for a handful of peppermint pig pellets.

The loading dock director, who raises colorful chickens for a hobby, claims Cunningham is bad to jump out from behind a pellet pallet and squeal real loud, hoping to make one of the men drop a bag or two.

I really can't see Cunningham acting that way, but that's what the man claims.

Still, I decided to look there first.

As he nearly always does, the loading dock director met me at the back door, inadvertently blocking my way.

"What do you want?" he asked.

"Nothing," I said. "I'm just here looking for my pet pig. He's run away from home again."

"Why did he run away from home again?"

"Because they put my picture in the paper instead of his."

"Well, that would do it."

"Is he here?"

"No."

"Are you sure?"

"It's hard to miss a pig."

Still determined to find Cunningham, I decided to search the north end of the county and assigned the south side to Judy.

We looked for more than a week, although I think my wife must have ridden with one of the neighbor ladies some because her car was always parked in the same spot whenever I got home.

Every day Cunningham was missing, I drove around the county yelling through an old bullhorn I picked up at a yard sale on our honeymoon years ago.

Turns out all my hollering wasn't necessary. (Neither was that "Disturbing the Peace" citation the Sheriff's deputy gave me, as far as I'm concerned.) Because the next week's newspaper had my pig's picture in it after all.

It was in an advertisement for a new barbecue joint up by Batesville, but Cunningham, bless his heart, didn't know the difference.

Somebody must have shown it to him because he came home the next day, fifty pounds lighter, but, otherwise, none the worse for wear.

To make sure the pig was okay, I took him to the hog hospital in Homer to see his pigiatrician. The pig doctor found some scratches on his hams but assured me they would cure nicely.

I know now I was just too hard on Cunningham. I mean, taking away his entertainment, and all. All that did was hurt his feelings. And I remember how I felt when my grandmother would punish me by hiding the Sears and Roebuck catalog a few weeks before Christmas every year.

Don't get me wrong. Grandmother may have been grumpy on the outside, but if you ever needed anything—like a good spanking—she'd be the first one there to give it to you.

Pigs can swim even without taking a lesson. In fact, there's an island in the Bahamas inhabited solely by swimming pigs. The place is appropriately called Pig Island. It is also known as Big Major Cay. The pigs even swim out to meet tourist boats.

If pigs aren't allowed, somebody ought to put up a sign

Much to the amazement of my wife, Judy, I was recently asked to speak at an important big-book event at the Decatur Library, which is located, as you might expect, in Decatur, Georgia.

When I noticed all the other authors who would be attending had much bigger books than mine, I became concerned. The biggest book I've ever written is only six-by-nine, and you have to round up the fractions to even get to that.

My goal is to someday write one large enough to fit comfortably on a coffee table, but I doubt it will ever happen. That's why my second goal is to become more optimistic. I haven't made much progress on that, but I keep telling myself I'm off to a good start.

My wife thought the invitation to that highfalutin Decatur affair must be a mistake.

But not me. In fact, I told her that unless that football player, who also happens to be named Emory Jones, had finally finished his autobiography, I didn't see how it could be.

With him having the exact same name, the post office understandably gets our mail mixed up all the time. I haven't said anything because he's paid our power bill twice, and who knows—lightning might strike three times.

I still can't explain why, but for some reason, Judy decided to come to Decatur with me. That may have been because I had promised her we'd stop by the place where Hollywood filmed the made-for-TV series *Ozark* while we were down that way. I've never seen it myself, but that's her favorite show.

Somebody said the filming location was somewhere behind the West Lake Waffle House, but, as I learned later, that's not the case.

Looking back, I probably should have told Judy that my pet pig, Cunningham, would be coming with us. But I was afraid she might not go if I did. You see, there's just not as much front-seat room in the truck when the pig sits up there, too.

But I felt the experience would be beneficial to Cunningham. Plus he could brag about it at next summer's pig camp. He had an awful time last year. The mud pit was dry, and the directors refused to let anybody hose it down due to the so-called drought.

So, I let Cunningham hide under a tarp behind the seat until we were finally on final for that big intersection north of Atlanta. I understand the locals call it Spaghetti Junction.

Anyway, that's when the pig raised up so he could see out.

I have to say, Judy was a good sport about it. She even scooted way over by the door to make room for the pig.

You'd think they'd have some good restaurants around a place called Spaghetti Junction, but the thing comes up on you so fast, you don't even get much of a chance to look, let alone stop.

Like most pigs his age, Cunningham loves roller coasters. And since he'd only seen the ones on television, he mistook Spaghetti Junction for one of those.

Despite Judy's protests, the pig's squeals of delight persuaded me to steer back over the interchange three times. I never did spot any good restaurants, though.

I would have gone across one more time, but Judy came down with that swimmy-headed headache she sometimes gets when we travel together. So, I finally got off and found one of those eight-lane affairs that passes for a side street in Decatur.

While we were stopped at a red light, I thought it might be a good idea to ask for directions. But the lady in the Lexus alongside us must have been hard of hearing because she kept staring straight ahead. I even tried pounding on the side of the truck door to get her attention.

I guess her window wouldn't roll down, and she was embarrassed about it. I mean, with her car being a Lexus and all.

When the light changed, I waved her on and tried to get one of the next cars in line to stop. When nobody did, I finally had to turn left from the center lane.

"You just made an illegal left turn," my wife pointed out, helpfully.

"It's okay," I replied. "That police car behind us just did the same thing."

When the policeman indicated he'd like to chat for a minute, I pulled over.

"Thanks for stopping," I said. "Nobody else would. Can you direct us to the library in Decatur? I believe it's called the Decatur Library."

I figured it must be downtown because that's where the officer told somebody on the police radio he was bringing us.

Not wanting to trouble him further, I pulled back on the road while he was busy with the radio. I have four-wheel drive, but his vehicle mired up in the median pretty bad when he tried to follow us.

Evidently, Decatur gets a lot of rain.

I felt terrible about not helping him get unstuck, but we were running late. Besides, I hadn't brought my chain with me.

When we finally found the place, Judy opted to stay in the truck—because of her headache, I guess—while Cunningham and I raced inside just as it came my turn to speak. Talk about good timing!

All went well until they handed me the microphone. Cunningham mistook it to be one of those electric cattle prods he'd seen used on his daddy once. So, he charged the stage to keep the same thing from happening to me, bless his heart.

My attorney has advised me not to talk about what happened next until after the hearing.

But I will say this: Decatur has some unusually harsh laws regarding pigs.

And the folks at the West Lake Waffle House claim to have never even heard of *Ozark*.

I'm not sure they were telling the truth.

But I have to admit, they never once waffled on their answer.

Taking your pig to
a concert can be tricky

As is true with lots of folks around here, local music legend Katie Deal and Patsy Cline are my pet pig Cunningham's all-time favorite singers. He loves them better than slop.

At one time, Cunningham had a girl pig friend named Pickles that he may have liked a little better. But they broke up after Pickles got picked up on a littering charge over by the tracks in Lula.

Cunningham took the break-up hard, especially after he learned half that litter wasn't even his. Truth is, he's still not over Pickles. Probably never will be.

So, you can imagine how pleased I was when I heard Katie was going to sing Patsy's songs up at the Hardman Farm State Historic Site just outside Helen.

But, before I could surprise him, Cunningham came trotting home with the neighbor's damp newspaper in his mouth, squealing the tidings himself.

I'll never forget how happy he looked. That pig was in hog heaven, I tell you, and determined to be at that concert with bells on. Cunningham wouldn't even let me finish my ham sandwich before insisting we order our tickets.

If you have a pet pig yourself, as so many now do, you know how pig-headed they can be; it's endearing, really. Although I think men appreciate that characteristic in a hog more than women do. At least that's been my experience.

Before long, Cunningham was hogging my computer, trying to type in the concert's innerweb address with a peppermint pig pellet. That might have worked, too, if they still put as much molasses in pig pellets as they used to.

Anyway, I decided to step in and order the tickets myself, since Cunningham can't remember my wife's credit card numbers as well as I can.

I typed in Cunningham's name as Cunningham P. Jones, and even added a little note explaining the "P" stood for pig. That was to avoid the type of bias that occasionally occurs whenever you try to buy any kind of ticket for a pig.

It's sad, but it's a fact of life pig owners learn to live with. The airlines are the worst.

I also noted on the concert ticket page that we'd like to sit near the stage while staying in as close proximity to the porta-potty as possible. Then I let Cunningham hit the send button with his soggy pig pellet.

The next morning about ten-thirty, the phone rang. It woke everybody in the house except my wife, who'd already left for her job at one of those big box stores—I forget which one.

"Hello," I said sleepily. "Who is this?"

"This is the President of the Concert Committee. Did you just attempt to purchase a ticket for a pig? Because there's been a complaint."

"Did my wife file it?"

"No. Not this time. But you most certainly may not bring your pig to our concert."

"Why not?"

"Because this thing is at the Hardman Farm State Historic Site! Even the governor is coming, for goodness' sake!"

The President of the Concert Committee had just hoisted himself on his own leotard.

"Exactly!" I said, sitting up in bed. "The key word here is *farm*, and nobody can ban a pig from one of those, not even the president of a concert committee."

I wasn't sure about a governor. But I didn't say anything.

"Are you sure?" he asked.

"I just looked it up."

I was bluffing, but he didn't know that. At least, I hoped not.

He must not have, because the man changed his tune pretty darn quick. He even said if I'd drop Cunningham off at his office the day before the concert, he'd make sure the pig got dressed out properly for the performance.

After that, he said Cunningham could ride to the show in some sort of special food truck the concert committee had rented for the occasion.

As tempting as he made it all sound, I was not going to take him up on his offer. Because anybody who spends a whole day dressing a pig is just wasting time. All you need to do is hose them down some and maybe tie a bandana around their neck if the event is formal.

When Saturday finally got here, that's precisely what I did. Of course, the pig and I had to listen to the entire concert from the horse barn because they never did send those tickets we ordered.

But, then again, they never did charge Judy's credit card for them either. If they had, she would have said something— believe me.

Call me crazy, but I just couldn't let Cunningham miss hearing Katie Deal sing those Patsy Cline songs.

No, sir. Not even if it took walkin' in after midnight—which it did, by the way.

Because to let Cunningham miss that concert would have been so wrong.

He might just fall to pieces.

People who know such things say there are more than two billion pigs on the planet. China has the most with 446,422,605. The United States is second with 65,909,002. Denmark has the honor of having more pigs than humans—2.15 pigs per person, to be exact.

Pig TV

I recently bought my pet pig, Cunningham, a television of his own.

Like my wife, Judy, you probably think I should have done that a long time ago. And, if you do, you're right. But I'm bad to procrastinate when it comes to putting things off.

Judy finally got fed up with Cunningham hogging her remote. Plus, she was tired of watching reruns of *Babe: Pig in the City*.

I read somewhere they were having a big Groundhog Day sale at that furniture store down in Flowery Branch. So, I loaded Cunningham in the truck and headed out.

As I expected it would be, the place was packed with holiday shoppers. Still, we found the television section without even asking directions.

I think the furniture store manager could tell we were serious customers because he came over right away. He even stood and watched while Cunningham and I tested the various models by turning them on and off real fast.

When it comes to electronics, that's the equivalent of thumping a watermelon. At least, according to my cousin, Wayne.

"Do you want to buy a television set?" the furniture store manager asked.

He was talking to me, but, for some reason, the man kept looking at Cunningham.

"Is that the only way they come?" I asked back. "Because we just need one. It's for my pig."

"Your pig?"

"Yes. Can you recommend something that would look good to a pig's eye? Black and white is fine. Especially if it's cheaper."

"You want a black and white TV for your pig?"

"I do. He's colorblind. Paying extra for pigment would be a waste of money."

"Your pig is colorblind?"

"Yep. He can't tell a yellow ear of corn from a blue one."

"And he watches television?"

"Way too much if you ask me, but what are you going to do in this day and age? Anyway, my wife and I want the pig to have one of his own. She's fed up with him always watching hers."

While the furniture store manager and I bantered back and forth about the various television models, Cunningham hopped up on a marked-down sofa. The marketing people had prudently positioned that discounted couch in front of a demo model TV playing the *Three Little Pigs* movie over and over.

They probably put that on when they saw Cunningham coming.

But I switched the darn thing off as soon as I noticed.

"What did you do that for?" asked the furniture store manager, somewhat crossly I thought.

I decided to chalk his crossness up to the holiday stress he had to be under.

"That *Three Little Pigs* flick is fun for us people," I told him firmly. "But to a hog, it's a horror flick. He'll have nightmares about it for a month."

The man didn't seem to care much.

"I don't care much," he said, confirming my suspicions. Then he turned the big screen back on.

I started to tell him I had an Agricultural Journalism Degree from the University of Georgia but thought better of it at the last minute.

"Oh, sure," I said. "You're not the one who'll have to get up tonight and read "The Three Little Wolves and the Big Bad Pig" for an hour to get him back to sleep."

"Don't you have a pig pen for him?"

"I did," I replied. "But the darn thing ran out of ink. Now he just uses a pencil."

I guess the furniture store manager was in a big hurry to serve other customers because he promptly sold us a color TV for the same price as a black and white model.

That was fine with me—there's no need to buy the whole hog when you just need a little sausage.

He even carried it out to the truck for us at no extra charge.

Cunningham was so excited he jumped up and down and cried wee, wee, wee all the way home. He weed a little on the truck seat, too, although I hope to get that cleaned up before my wife notices.

Once Judy got the new television hooked up, I wrapped Cunningham in a blanket and settled him down to watch *The Pigtail Chronicles* on the Prime Pork channel.

I would have watched it with him, but my doctor says I should get off the couch more. So, now I only watch television in bed.

I don't know how people managed before TV came along. I asked my grandmother once what her parents did for entertainment before television.

She said she didn't know.

Then I asked each of her eight sisters and nine brothers, and they didn't know either.

Many people collect piggy banks. Seriously. And not just for the coins they hold. In the Middle Ages, people stored money in an orange-colored container made from clay called "pygg." Soon, "pygg" evolved into "pig." Somebody added a slot, and the rest is history.

Trailgate

I understand the newspapers are already calling this affair "Trailgate."

It all started when my pet pig, Cunningham, found a brochure promoting that new footpath from the Hardman Farm State Historic Site to downtown Helen, Georgia—the place everybody calls an Alpine village.

Personally, I think the town is way too large to be called a village anymore. But that's just me.

Anyway, it's not pertinent here.

Cunningham was tickled pink because the brochure said the route ran along an old pig trail somebody or other had later turned into a railroad bed. The whole thing runs alongside the Chattahoochee River, which—to Cunningham—meant plenty of mud.

That made him as happy as two pigs in a gunny sack.

Always a go-getter, Cunningham decided right then and there he would become the first pig in history to walk that new trail.

And to make sure he truly *was* the first, he decided to make his walk on opening day.

I don't know when I've been prouder of a pig.

Even my wife, Judy, liked the idea. Although I think that was mostly because it would get Cunningham out of the house for a while. That way, she could do a little deep cleaning.

When Cunningham heard the governor was coming up for the event, the pig got so excited he didn't eat for an hour. That hadn't happened since the folks down at the hog hospital in Homer gave him that de-worming pill last fall.

Even so, Cunningham made plans for the governor and those other dignitaries to walk up the trail behind him on his historic march. He even intended to wave a little flag while everybody strolled along.

The pig practiced for hours. However, I never did get through to the governor's office to tell them about Cunningham's arrangements.

Still, once the big day came, there were cars in the parking lot from as far away as Franklin County. Later, we found out that Franklin County lady had taken a wrong turn in Cleveland, but she was there, nonetheless.

When Cunningham heard on the radio that the governor would arrive in a state-issued helicopter, we both wrongly assumed he would land on the Indian Mound over by the river.

So, Cunningham hid up under the mound's little gazebo with his flag, to wait.

We later learned the airspace over that mound is restricted, even for the governor. But who knew?

Certainly not the mayor of Sautee. He buzzed the mound twice before landing right beside it.

Show-off.

When Peach Force One touched down—as we now know it properly should have—in the hayfield across the road from the mound, it threw Cunningham's timing off.

Plus, those dumb black-and-white cows in the pasture thought the helicopter was dropping alfalfa pellets for them. So, they all lined up by the fence, blocking Cunningham's path, which made it even more problematic for him to cross the road.

For a chicken, it would have been a disaster.

By the time the pig made it over, the governor's people were driving him up in a caravan of two black SUVs. Cunningham inadvertently, and understandably, mistook the whole thing for a funeral procession.

To show his respect for what he thought was the dearly departed—something I've tried to instill in him over the years—the pig slowly lowered his flag.

Regrettably, those men in dark suits misjudged his intentions. In their defense, that little grommet on the end of the flagpole does look dangerous.

To try and resolve the issue, the men in black flashed their State-of-Georgia-issued Secret Service lookalike badges. This, naturally, made Cunningham think those people must be the escorts for his soon-to-be historic trail walk.

But when the gentleman in front yelled through his megaphone for the pig to, and I quote here, "TAKE A HIKE," Cunningham started running up the trail as fast as he could.

A rumor spread that a charity race had broken out. And with there being so many politicians in one place during an election year, things got spirited fast. Most of the crowd started running up the trail behind the pig, heading for Helen like Friday night had come early.

Luckily, a photographer sent up his camera drone so the local radio station could cover—what could now only be called a race—from the ground.

At the finish line, a Helen official correctly called Cunningham the winner.

That lady from Franklin County came in second.

The governor himself chose not to participate. I imagine that's because he'd campaigned against pig racing during the last election, and it would have looked bad for him.

Cunningham had no sooner crossed the finish line than the man with the bullhorn whisked him off to the helicopter. I figured they wanted to use the pig for political endorsements or some such down in Atlanta.

In fact, that very next night, I saw the pig on television with the governor at a watermelon-cutting festival in Cordele.

He'll be home soon enough, though, because—believe me—that pig is not cut out for politics.

None of them are, really.

Still, I'm proud to say Cunningham was the first pig to run the Helen to Hardman Heritage Trail. Not only that, but he did it in a still unbroken time of four minutes and four seconds.

I wish they'd put a little plaque up to commemorate that, but with state funding being what it is these days, I doubt they ever will.

The Read-Between-the-Wines Book Club and Play Society

After being boorishly booted from several area book clubs that are far too restrictive to swine, my pet pig, Cunningham, and I decided to start our own—the Read-Between-the-Wines Book Club and Play Society.

Early on, it was just the pig and me. It could have stayed that way if Cunningham hadn't insisted on making *If You Give a Pig a Pancake* our book selection three months in a row. Oh, sure, it's a classic, but all that talk about maple syrup gets sticky after a while.

So, I talked my cousin, Wayne, and his girlfriend, Viola Mae, into joining our new book club, too. I believe Viola Mae, who claims to have read the entire innerweb twice, shows up more for the wine than the reading, though.

But as Wayne says, just because she's bad to get drunk and shoot guns in the air doesn't make her any less a lady.

It's not really Viola Mae's fault—she grew up in a town so small they didn't have a town drunk. So, everybody had to take turns.

Now, don't get me wrong. Wayne usually doesn't drink all that much himself. That's because after a couple glasses of wine, he turns into a completely different person. And that person drinks a LOT!

Last month, our book club had its first guest speaker—renowned reader and writer Dr. Percy Niles of Smyrna.

Now, I may have inflated our book club's participation numbers a tiny bit in my invitation letter. But, in my defense, Wayne and I had a massive membership drive planned. I really did think we'd be well over a hundred by the time Dr. Niles came to speak.

But even so, talking to a small group would still give the man a chance to promote his newest book, *A Fellow Called Othello*.

As a pre-meeting reading assignment, he'd sent up a play called *Hamlet*. None of us had time to read it, though.

Our club meets in the back of Wayne's muffler repair shop out on Highway 115, and after we watched Dr. Niles drive past the place several times, he finally pulled in.

"Welcome to the Read-Between-the-Wines Book and Play Society," I said formally. "Care for a shot of merlot?"

"Is that a pig?" asked Dr. Niles, pointing to Cunningham. Clearly, the man was a city slicker.

"Yes, sir, it is. That's my pet pig, Cunningham. He's excited about discussing *Hamlet*. You can see why—I mean, with him being a pig and all."

"Where is everyone?" Dr. Niles asked when he noticed Wayne and Viola Mae were the only other people in the muffler repair shop.

Always quick on my feet, I said, "Oh, our secretary inadvertently put the wrong date in the newsletter. Everybody thinks you're coming tomorrow. I would have called, but I didn't have your number handy."

Dr. Niles sighed and asked if we'd all read this *Hamlet* play by somebody named William Shakespeare.

"Everybody has but the pig," I white lied. "He had a busy week."

"Well, what's your impression of the piece?"

Wayne and Viola Mae just stared into their plastic wine glasses. Cunningham was busy sniffing an empty Coke can Wayne had left on the floor, so I spoke up first.

"It was nice."

Dr. Niles looked a bit confused. "Nice? Why, *Hamlet* is Shakespeare's finest work. That's why I featured it so prominently in my *A Fellow Called Othello* book, which I will be happy to autograph at the end of the meeting."

Trying to appear interested—the man *had* driven all the way from Smyrna, bless his heart—I asked, "Has this Shakespeare fellow written anything else?"

For some reason, the question irritated our speaker. "Have you never heard of *Macbeth*?"

I thought for a minute. "I think there was a McBeth family over on Shoal Creek one time. They moved to Buford, though. Or maybe it was Hiawassee."

Dr. Niles rubbed his face with both hands. "Shakespeare's magnificent play, *Macbeth,* is staged somewhere in the world every four hours."

"Holy Moly!" I said. "That must be awfully hard on the cast."

Dr. Niles muttered something or other about this whole thing being like a midsummer night's dream. Which was odd, since this was November.

That made me remember my eighth-grade teacher talking about some fellow from England who wrote stuff sorta like this. So, I decided to ask what I hoped was an appropriate question on the matter.

"Didn't this Mack Beth fellow stab some guy named Romeo?"

"No. Romeo killed himself."

"Why?"

"Because he thought his Juliet had died."

"Oh. Had she been sick?"

Dr. Niles suddenly remembered another meeting he'd forgotten back in Smyrna. That was probably good because Viola Mae had downed just enough box-wine to make her reach for the twelve-gauge.

The man drove away so fast, I don't think he even heard her two-blast sendoff.

Dr. Niles even forgot to take the little parting gift Cunningham was holding for him in his mouth.

Oh, well.

All's well that ends well, I guess.

When pigs fly

I've always enjoyed flying, but only in small airplanes. Those big ones scare me.

Of course, my neighbor and high-time pilot, Chuck Jägermeister, always claims aviation is the only industry in the world with a perfect record. "We've never left one up there yet," he points out every time the subject of airplanes comes up.

But I still worry. Take my last flight, for example. When we still hadn't left the gate after an hour, I asked the flight attendant what the problem was.

"Oh, the pilot thought he heard a funny noise in one of the engines," she said. "I guess it's taking them a while to find another pilot."

While we're on the subject of air travel, I want to confess that a recent aviation incident at our local dirt strip may have inadvertently been my fault.

Actually, it was the fault of my pet pig, Cunningham. But as anyone responsible for the actions of a pig will tell you, the truck stops here. And now that the three-month statute of limitations has expired, I want to land this thing out in the open.

It all started because my pig was upset that The Old Sautee Tea Room and Pig Food Store had recently raised the price of those peppermint pig pellets they sell up there. The newspaper said the increase was necessary because of the recent spike in peppermint prices, but who knows?

Anyhow, Cunningham started carrying a little price-increase protest sign back and forth in front of the establishment. And, as I expected might happen, their loading dock director, who raises colorful chickens as a hobby, soon gave me a call.

"Do you know your pig is up here carrying a protest sign?"

"I do. He painted it himself."

"I can tell."

"Yes. I thought it looked good, too. Especially when you consider that nobody around here will let him take art lessons."

"Well, I don't like it."

"I don't like it either. But every studio we've talked to has refused to sign the pig up."

"No. I mean, I don't like his protest sign."

"Why? He didn't use profanity again, did he?"

The man hesitated before admitting, "I'm not sure. It's in pig Latin."

"I told him that was a mistake."

"Just tell me what he's protesting."

"He's upset you raised the price of peppermint pig pellets. You can't blame him, either. I mean, he is on a fixed income."

The loading dock director sighed. At least that's what it sounded like over the phone, although there was an awful lot of road noise.

But then he said clearly, "We had to do that. Peppermint prices have gone through the roof. Surely, he's heard about that on the news. Besides, our pig pellets only went up two cents a bag."

This was true. I saw on the innerweb that some of the feed stores down around Pendergrass had raised theirs by a nickel.

Still, I felt the need to defend my pig. "We don't let Cunningham watch much news. It gives him the hives."

"Listen," said the loading dock director, who, for some reason, sounded annoyed. "What's it going to take to get this pig off my back?"

"You'll have to ask him."

"Do what? I'd look silly talking to a pig."

"No, you won't. I do it all the time, and nobody's ever thought I look silly. Except my wife. And the neighbors. But I think they were just teasing."

The loading dock director sighed again. "I'm not talking to a pig, and that's final."

"Okay then," I said, trying to be the adult here. "Put him on the phone."

"Put who on what?"

I guess all the road noise made it hard for him to hear, too. "Put my pig on your telephone so I can talk to him. But you'll need to hold it up."

"The phone?"

"No. His ear. It's hard for him to hear if you don't." Clearly, the man has never spent much time around pigs.

Once they got the phone situated, I asked Cunningham what it would take to call off his protest. The pig doesn't actually talk, mind you, but I've learned to interpret his snorts and grunts pretty accurately. In fact, Swine-ese has almost become a second language to me.

"Snort," he grunted.

"Are you serious?" I asked back, surprised at Cunningham's demand. "I don't know if he'll go for that."

"Grunt," Cunningham snorted. I could tell he meant it, too.

"All right then. Put the man back on."

"Well?" asked the loading dock director. "What does he want?"

"He's heard you're a pilot. That's true isn't it?"

"Well, yeah, in my spare time."

"Okay. Cunningham wants to buzz Clermont."

"What?"

"He wants to buzz Clermont."

"You mean, in an airplane?"

"How else would a pig buzz Clermont? Only, it has to be in one of those little ultra-lights. The smaller the better, really.

"What?" he asked.

"Larger planes scare him. I'm afraid he gets that from me."

"Absolutely not!"

"Okay. But he's gonna keep marching. And it never looks good for a pig food store to have a pig protesting in front of it."

Seeing his options were limited, the loading dock director finally gave in. "All right then. Meet me at the Clermont airstrip. But you'd better not tell anybody about this."

"Agreed," I said. "Be sure to let Cunningham ride up front. He's bad to get carsick in the back seat."

By the time we all got to the dirt strip, Cunningham was so excited his little pig's feet were dancing.

"How much does the pig weigh?" asked the loading-dock-director-turned-pilot. "I mean, dressed out for flying."

Cunningham is sensitive about his weight, so I crossed my fingers and shaved a hundred or so pounds off the real number. I figured it was just a record-keeping thing, anyhow.

Turns out it wasn't.

Cunningham and the loading-dock-director-turned-pilot were both squealing at a high-pitched volume long before they ever hit that big kudzu patch at the end of the runway.

Thankfully, nobody got hurt, but I doubt that ultralight's ever gonna fly again. At least not well.

As I told the FAA lady later, fudging the pig's weight may have been a mistake on my part.

Still, I think Cunningham and the loading dock director both learned a valuable lesson about gravity that day.

Because when it comes to airplanes, ladders and Dolly Parton on a trampoline, gravity never loses—the best you can hope for is a draw.

But I'll tell you one thing—pigs will fly before Cunningham gets in another airplane.

Even a small one.

Consider the warthog. I mean, why not? They're pigs, too. And, yes, warthogs do have warts of a sort, although they're actually just bumps of fleshy, thick skin. Female warthogs find these warts quite attractive on the male. The bigger, the better. To each his own, I guess.

Christmas shopping for a pig

Last Christmas, despite my wife, Judy's, concerns about the matter, I was determined to get my pet pig, Cunningham, something special to put under his tree.

Since Christmas is the Season of Good Will, that store is where I usually do my shopping. But I wanted this year to be different.

The truth is I needed to make up for the gag gift I so thoughtlessly gave Cunningham last year. It was a pack of double A batteries with a little note attached that read, "Toy not included."

I thought it was hilarious, but he didn't. Especially since he'd blown half his allowance to get me a full can of Pringles. He even paid extra for the sour cream and onion ones, bless his heart.

To make matters worse, my wife wasn't thrilled with her present, either. I thought for sure she'd get excited over one of those cool, over-sized flyswatters that were all the rage back then.

I think it was because a flyswatter is more of a summertime gift.

A do-it-yourself exercise and weight-loss book from the year before hadn't gone over as well as I'd hoped, either. And while you'd think, as I did, nothing says loving like a gift certificate for a shingles shot, you'd be wrong.

So, this year, I went all out with two pairs of extra-thick waterproof socks and a hardback edition of the new *Fifty Shades of Chicken* cookbook. I can't wait to see the look on her face when she opens those!

Holiday shopping has always been challenging for me. Especially the Christmas one. Easter is easy—boil a few eggs, and you're home free. So is National Nothing Day. (It's a real holiday—look it up if you don't believe me. At least it was at the time of this writing.)

But, other than those, I think seasonal shopping is hard on everybody. A while back, I saw a family doing their Christmas shopping down at the store. They were pushing and shoving and yelling, "Get me this!" "I want that!" "Buy that one!"

Their kids were even worse.

Even so, I wanted to get Cunningham a present that would make his little pig eyes sparkle. Now, if you're going to buy your dog, your cat, or even your pet skunk, a gift, the world is your oyster. But—and this is so sad— it's slim pickings when it comes to pig presents.

I finally decided to go easy on myself and give Cunningham a three-dollar gift certificate to his favorite place—The Old Sautee Tea Room and Pig Food Store. That way, he could pick out his own present, and there'd be no skin off my back if he didn't like it.

Cunningham's tail was all but wagging when we arrived at the store the day after Christmas.

Before I even got parked good, he rooted the door open and raced inside with hybrid vigor. (That's a pork term in case you don't have an Agricultural Journalism Degree from the University of Georgia like I do.)

Cunningham was halfway down the pet-food aisle when I walked through the door.

The loading dock director, who raises colorful chickens for a hobby, was in the back room grooming his prize pet rooster, Sir Randolph Scott. The cockerel crowed when he saw us, although the sun had already been up for hours.

Stupid chicken.

"Is that your pig on our pet-food aisle?" the loading dock director asked, using his management voice.

"Yes. He's Christmas shopping. I got him a gift certificate for Christmas this year."

"A what?"

"A gift certificate. In the amount of three dollars."

"Three dollars?"

"Yes. I didn't want to go whole hog on it. There's nothing worse than a spoiled pig, you know."

"He needs to leave."

"Why?"

"Pigs aren't allowed in here."

"You don't have a sign saying so. Besides, this is a pig food store. You should be begging hogs to come in here. That's just marketing 101."

Right then, Cunningham ran up to the counter with a "Sing-Along with Swine" CD filled with Christmas songs by legendary pigs like Miss Piggy, Babe and Porky. My favorite was a duet sung by Arnold and Eb from that timeless television classic, *Green Acres*.

He must have found it on the bottom shelf with some other marked-down items beside the corn kernels.

"Is this what you want?" I asked. I already knew it was because the CD had Miss Piggy on the cover.

Cunningham grunted yes and dropped his soggy gift certificate by the checkout counter.

The total came to $2.95, so the girl gave Cunningham a nickel back, which the pig swallowed for safekeeping.

The song collection was actually pretty good. It featured hogs hollering hits like "Have Yourself a Muddy Little Christmas," "Hamming it Up for the Holidays," and "Grandma Got Run Over in our Pigsty."

Once you hear that last one, it keeps running through your head all day long.

Many Chinese people associate pigs with fertility. In fact, Chinese couples hoping to have children often keep a pig picture or symbol around to bring them luck in this matter. My wife says that's hogwash. But who knows? There are a lot of Chinese.

In a small town,
wearing underwear is essential

The only drawbacks I've found to living in the country are the occasional rabid skunk and the fact that small-town newspapers know way too much about what goes on.

They'll publish things like the police reports, traffic stops—even your mama's squash recipe if they can get their hands on it.

Except for those recipes, they put most things like that in a section called *The Blotter*. In fact, lots of folks read *The Blotter* before they read anything else. I know I do. My wife may not, though—I'm not sure.

Pigs like *The Blotter*, too. In fact, it's the favorite part of the paper for my pet pig, Cunningham, next to the grocery store ads, of course.

Newspapers rarely name names in *The Blotter*. They don't have to. In a small town, everybody knows who and what they're writing about.

For example, I was talking to my wife, Judy, about a piece in *The Blotter* just the other day. "Did you see where ole man

Honeyhopper got caught taking eggs from Aunt Lizzie's hen house again the other morning?"

"Yeah," said Judy. "I read about that in *The Blotter*. They said this was the third time this month, and that she threatened to shoot a load of rock salt into his backside if he does it again. Still, the deputy let him off with a warning. It also mentioned he'd been drinking."

The paper had only written, "Two dozen eggs stolen from Asbestos Road henhouse."

That's why a recent story in *The Blotter* about my cousin Wayne hit so close to home. His mama never will get over it. Me either, since it inadvertently involved Cunningham, too.

It stated that a Sheriff's deputy made a "male citizen" jump up and down on one foot to prove he was sober. That caused the suspect's pants to fall down, revealing he wasn't wearing underwear. It also noted this "male citizen" had been drinking and had two pigs in his car.

Well, everybody knew right off it was Wayne because he prides himself on not wearing a belt, suspenders or underwear. He claims it's too inconvenient—especially during the summer months. He will sometimes put on a belt if it gets cold enough, though.

And the only pigs he's ever had in his car are his pet pig, Jerry Lee, and Cunningham. Wayne had volunteered to take the two of them to the hog hospital in Homer for their annual rhinitis booster shots to save me the trip. So, I'd dropped Cunningham off at Wayne's house the night before for a sleepover.

Everybody and their brother knew about it.

Since Cunningham was in the car at the time of Wayne's unfortunate incarceration, my aunt—Wayne's mama—asked me to visit my cousin and the two pigs in jail. She even slipped me a few bucks for bail money.

I immediately posted the three-dollar bail fee for each of the pigs. I later learned they would not have been arrested at all if they'd just kept their snouts shut. But what are you gonna do?

I decided it might be good to let ole Wayne cool his heels in the slammer for a few days. At least until he came up with that ten bucks he owed me, anyway.

Plus, it gave the two of us a chance to chat.

Wayne convinced me the whole affair was a big misunderstanding.

As they say in Hollywood, here's the backstory. You see, the night before he was to head for Homer, someone removed all four tires, wheels and all, from his classic 1966 Ford Fairlane.

That was a real shame because, while Wayne's Fairlane has pretty high mileage, it still runs. Occasionally.

So, before heading to Homer with the hogs, Wayne—always safety-conscious—thought it would be best if he got the Fairlane over to Tito's Tires and Toenails in Toccoa first. That's where his mama gets her nails done.

It's also the place where he had that coupon his mama gave him last Christmas for four brand new retreads.

While Wayne always has a few spare rims lying around, he didn't have the funds to hire a rollback. So, being handy about such things, he dug up three tires from the flower bed. Then he got down the one he'd tossed on the roof last winter to hold down a piece of loose tin.

Then he and Viola Mae installed all four on the Fairlane. After borrowing a little gas money from her, Wayne loaded up the pigs and headed out.

Everything went well until the three of them turned onto the paved road.

That's when the tire that had been on the roof blew out. I guess that thing was pretty weathered from all the sun. Plus, I saw Jerry Lee up there sleeping on it last winter, and nothing damages synthetic rubber like a pig on a cold tin roof.

With both pigs sticking their heads out opposite windows to spot for him, Wayne was trying to maneuver the Fairlane to the side of the road, and still avoid that big gully at the same time, when the deputy happened by. Isn't that always the way?

A key part of the story is that Wayne has put on a few pounds over the past few years. That's due to a thyroid condition that causes him to crave cream-filled Ho Hos. His mama has the same thing.

But Wayne had recently signed up for one of those weight-loss plans where they mail food to you whenever they think you might be getting hungry. As a result, he's dropped more than three-and-one-half pounds in eight months. I think most of that came from walking back and forth to the mailbox, but still, we're all proud of him.

Naturally, considering that recent weight loss, jumping up and down on one foot caused his pants to fall—that's just gravity at work.

As for not wearing underwear, well, like I said, that's just Wayne.

He also had a good explanation as to why the deputy smelled alcohol on his breath. You see, it was an unusually warm afternoon. So, he and Viola Mae had shared a mango wine cooler while she helped him install those four tires on the Fairlane.

Having been on a mail-order diet for so long, that wine cooler hit Wayne hard.

As I intend to testify at the trial, the mere fact that Wayne could jump up and down on one foot long enough for his pants to fall down proves he wasn't sloshed.

I bet the judge can't do that—sober *or* tipsy.

While he may not buy my story, thankfully, Wayne's mama will, bless her heart.

The moral is, if you live in a small town, don't allow your pig to stick his head out the window, keep good tires on your car and always wear underwear.

I don't think they still arrest people for not wearing undies in our larger towns now, but I can't be sure.

So, be careful out there.

Toilet paper is on a roll but I'm wiped out

Nobody who lived through it will soon forget The Great Coronavirus Toilet Paper Shortage of 2020. There hasn't been anything like it since that run on toothpaste during the Solar Tsunami of 1984.

Speaking of toothpaste, since dentists make their money off bad teeth, why on earth would anybody buy a brand of that stuff four out of five dentists recommend using? I'm just saying.

I understand the run on toilet paper started from a poorly worded RFD-TV report. It stated that the first noticeable symptom of this new virus that was going around was the backdoor trots.

It turns out the story had actually been about a sporadic turkey disease with a similar name. But you know how rumors hang on once they get put out there.

I didn't realize the seriousness of the sanitation situation until my wife, Judy's, birthday rolled around again. That's when one of her friends, for a birthday present, sent her a three-pack of single-ply toilet tissue, gift-wrapped.

Judy was so touched, she teared up. Then she had me go to the bank to put one of the rolls in our safe-deposit box.

Turns out my pet pig, Cunningham, and I had both inadvertently forgotten Judy's birthday. So, we figured, since we were in town anyway, we might as well wait for a Brinks truck carrying toilet paper to show up at the store.

I'd heard on the scanner one was on the way, under escort.

Once it arrived, we planned to stand in line long enough to buy Judy a roll or two of two-ply and come out of this thing smelling like a rose. I knew there would be long lines, but I've learned lines can move pretty fast when you have a pig by your side.

Since face masks were as scarce as toilet paper back then, Judy had shrewdly made two of them out of one of her old double-breasted brassieres.

Cunningham naturally assumed one of those bra masks was for him, and I didn't have the heart to tell the pig otherwise. So, before we left, I gave him mine and grabbed that old ski mask I wear when it snows for myself. Then we headed for town.

When we got to the bank, the pig and I put on our masks, grabbed the birthday roll of TP and went inside. They really do treat you like a VIP there because, as soon as we walked in, the bank's manager rushed right up to us.

"May I help you?" he asked, looking as jumpy as a June bug in a hen house. I figured he must be new at the job.

"I suppose you know why we're here," I said, holding up Judy's roll of toilet paper.

Times being what they were, I supposed I wasn't the first person to put toilet paper in a safe-deposit box.

The man swallowed hard and nodded. "Yes. But what about the pig?"

I had to chuckle. "His mask isn't required by law, but we don't want anybody to get hurt, do we?"

"Just tell me what you want," the manager said, dabbing his forehead with a used deposit slip. "I'll do my best to make it happen."

"Toilet paper," I said. "It's my wife's birthday."

"You don't want money?"

"Well, this time last year, money might have been a good idea for her. But now, toilet paper seems like a better option."

The man nodded and swallowed even harder. He must have had a sore throat because, from the way he looked, I think he was coming down with something.

"I'll get that for you. Just wait right there. And don't bother anybody else while I'm gone. Please."

I was impressed. Most of the time, I can't even get anybody in there to make eye contact. I probably should have been going straight to the manager all along.

"Great," I said. "You really are a full-service bank! We'd prefer two-ply if you have it."

The manager ran into both bathrooms without knocking on either door and came back with several rolls.

"What else?" he asked, placing the toilet paper on that counter they keep the pens chained to.

"Well, I was going to put a roll in our safe-deposit box, but I guess there's no need now."

I reached for my wallet to pay, but he wasn't about to take money because he stuck both hands in the air and said, "No! Please! There's no need for that!"

"All right then," I said, picking up as many of the rolls as I could safely carry.

Just then, Cunningham grunted and made a move toward the bank manager, who raised his hands even higher. In a show of support, two tellers and at least one customer did the same thing.

"What does that hog want?" The man looked at Cunningham like he had a bomb strapped to his back or something. Plus, the bank manager's voice got so high, I thought he might be running a fever, too.

"Oh. I promised Cunningham I'd get him one of those little suckers you sometimes give to your larger depositors. Would that be alright?"

We must have more money in that bank than my wife lets on because that generous gentleman, sick as he was, set the entire jar of suckers in front of my pig.

A lot of banks won't even let animals come in.

His gesture touched me. It must have touched others, too. Because, by now, everybody there was staring at us.

The pig squealed his thanks and started rolling the jar toward the door with his bra-covered snout. However, in the process, his mask came off.

When it did, everybody averted their eyes. To avoid embarrassing the pig, I guess.

"Nobody saw his face!" the bank manager assured me. "I swear it!"

I wasn't sure why that mattered much, but I didn't say anything. Then I walked out backwards in front of the pig to make sure he didn't drop anything else.

Before getting to the car, we heard sirens off in the distance. I figured they must be blocking the road for the governor or something. I'd heard he was speaking to the Rotary Club that day. Or maybe it was Kiwanis.

So, not wanting to get tied up in traffic, we left in a hurry.

I still don't understand how all the stores in town could be out of toilet paper, and yet they were giving it away free down at the bank.

Oh, well. I guess it's just one of those supply-and-demand things.

Pig lands—then loses—rooster role

When I heard my pet pig, Cunningham, had been selected to be in a play, I was so proud I could mop.

That was supposed to be pop.

Stupid spell-check.

As much as I hate to brag, how many other people can say that about their pet pig?

Not many, I bet. At least once you get outside Arkansas and all those states that start with an "I" up there by the corn belt.

The play—set in my uncle Cheever's pottery shop when I was little—is appropriately enough, I guess, called *Cheever*. I originally wanted to name it *Uncle Cheever*, but rather than risk being fired for creative differences, I decided to let the producers win one for once.

I was tickled pink that Cunningham, after only a tiny bit of practice, landed the coveted role of Cheever's rooster, Joe.

Now, as you might imagine, landing the Joe role didn't come easy. That's mostly because the loading dock director at The

Ole Sautee Tea Room and Pig Food Store wanted his prize rooster, Sir Randolph Scott, to get the role, too.

Stupid chicken.

I've heard the same thing almost happened to Clark Gable in the first version of *Gone with the Wind*.

To keep it from happening here, Cunningham and I arrived early on audition day. By early, I mean early afternoon. Pigs are way too cranky in the morning to try out for much of anything, let alone a play. At least until they get their first cup of coffee grounds.

Nevertheless, just as we were pulling in, that prize rooster and his owner were pulling out.

After I moved over to let him pass, I stopped at the guard shack. "Where should I park?" I asked. "We're here for the *Cheever* tryouts.

The guard shined his flashlight inside my truck, even though it was broad daylight.

"Is that a pig?"

I could tell right off the man was a city slicker. "Yes," I said, shielding my eyes from his flashlight's light as best I could. "He wants to be a rooster, though. In the play, I mean. Would you like to hear him crow?"

"No need," said the guard. "Sir Randolph Scott just landed the rooster role a few minutes ago. He's such a natural I even cast the tiebreaker vote myself."

This news riled Cunningham so much that, bless his heart, he stuck his head out the window and crowed in disappointment.

But, despite his limited amount of practice time, that cock-a-doodle-do was the most magnificent crow that I, or anyone else for that matter, had ever heard a rooster crow. Let alone a pig.

Even the security guard got misty.

To make a long story longer, the director, who had just heard Cunningham's chicken imitation at the guard shack, ran outside, fired Sir Randolph Scott over the phone and immediately hired the pig.

When the play opened, early reviews were good. They got even better once the actors learned their lines.

Of course, since the Play Actors Guild didn't have time to properly vet Cunningham—it being his first performance, and all—his part had to be played entirely offstage. But when people heard ole Joe crow, they knew who it was doing the crowing.

And they jeered. Lord, how they jeered.

That was supposed to be cheered, not jeered.

Stupid spell-check.

Anyway, that's the good news. Now, let's fast-forward a few months for the bad.

The Sautee Nacoochee Cultural Center, which sits just to the right of Helen, Georgia, is about to put on the second performance of *Cheever*. This was for the folks who didn't get to see the play the first time because they sold out of tickets.

I told them they should have printed more tickets, but they didn't listen to me.

The reason they sold out of tickets was mostly because of my pet pig Cunningham's stellar performance as Joe the Rooster.

Naturally, the crowds were huge. People turn out in droves when they get a chance to see a pig play any sort of trans-species role. In theatre circles, that's known as the "swine swing effect."

So, naturally, Cunningham and I both assumed he'd again play the rooster in the *Cheever* rerun.

That is until he received an accredited letter from the director saying they were going, and I quote here, "in a new direction."

I knew right off the bat he planned to cast a real rooster this time instead of a pig. And, as I suspected, the chosen chicken was none other than Sir Randolph Scott, the prize rooster Cunningham completely crushed in last year's auditions.

Stupid chicken.

I smelled a rat. And even after I fished it out from under the refrigerator, I was still suspicious.

So was Cunningham.

Consequently, the pig and I headed for town. We soon spotted the play's director eating wings at a popular downtown restaurant with some guy named Clyde.

And, just as I suspected, the loading dock director for The Old Sautee Tea Room and Pig Food Store, who raises colorful chickens for a hobby, was sitting with them.

I left Cunningham in the truck—with the windows down, naturally—and went inside to confront the man. The play director, not Clyde. I don't even know him.

"I see some chicken has usurped my pig in the upcoming Cheever play," I said politely.

The play director and the loading dock director both stared at me. That was probably because they'd never heard me use the word "usurped" before.

Still, the play director finally nodded in the affirmative.

I stomped my foot to show I meant business. "Nobody will ever pay good money to see a rooster crow. It's just not right."

"Yes, it is."

"No, it's not."

"Says who?"

Then he pulled out a little black book and opened it to page three. "Says the Play Actors Guild rulebook." Then he pointed to directive number 101 dash B, subsection 23-A, part two, paragraph four, which was underlined in red ink.

I guess he'd done his homework because it plainly stated, "Only a chicken shall play the role of a rooster."

The play director had me there. I had no choice but to go back outside, which wasn't a bad move since it was a pleasant day, and all.

I'm not proud of what I did next. (Actually, I kinda am.) But there, in the back of the loading dock director's truck, sat Sir Randolph Scott, preening proudly in his gilded cage.

Stupid rooster.

Before I could even try to stop myself, I reached over and opened his gilded cage door. Cunningham grunted encouragement from the truck window.

"Shoo," I said. But the rooster wouldn't shoo. He just flapped his wings and glared at me.

Cunningham naturally took the wing-flapping to be a sign of aggression. So, he jumped out the window, raced over and crowed at the rooster in his best chicken voice.

Ashamed of being out-crowed by a pig, Sir Randolph Scott finally flew the coop. That fowl isn't much of a flyer, but he managed to make it to the top of a funnel cake truck headed for Helen.

When the play director saw his star rooster perched up there, he raced out—without paying his bill, I might add—to chase the funnel cake truck. So did the loading dock director.

Clyde just sat there, so I guess he got stuck with the bill.

Cunningham, squealing like a fig (stupid spell-check), gave chase, too. The last I saw of them, the rooster, the fig, the loading dock director and the funnel cake truck were all headed north.

It all ended well, though, because Cunningham's agent called the next day to say Hollywood had offered him a starring role in an upcoming remake of *Animal Farm*.

By that, I mean, they had offered the role to the agent, not to Cunningham.

But we were both incredibly happy for the man.

At least I was.

Cunningham wants me to start looking for him a new agent.

Getting your pig in
a play is never a shoo-in
(even if you wrote the darn thing)

After my pet pig, Cunningham, caught all kinds of praise for his role of Joe the Rooster in that long-way-off-Broadway production of *Cheever*, he really got infected by the acting bug.

So, when he caught wind that Piedmont College over in Demorest, Georgia, was putting on a play based on my book, *The Valley Where They Danced*, he naturally wanted to have a role in that one, too.

We both figured he'd be a shoo-in for a nice part. After all, he'd even helped write the darn thing. By that, I mean he ate a copy of the manuscript I'd inadvertently left on the porch one night—binder and all.

And, with Cunningham having digested so much of the material, no one could say he didn't have pigskin in the game.

So, we incorrectly assumed getting the pig a part would not be a problem. But, as it turns out, only pigs with links to the close-knit Thespian Nation have any pull when it comes to casting.

In fact, they wouldn't even let Cunningham on the couch.

Now, he never expected the leading role. That part required kissing the costar, and well, let's face it, finding anybody willing to kiss a pig on the mouth is hard. It has been ever since the Great Recession ended.

Besides, pigs are mostly cast as minor character actors now days, and he's good with that.

No, the role he wanted was the part of the dog.

In this play, the canine's name is Jack, so to help get into character, Cunningham insisted I call him "Jack" from then until casting day.

My wife, Judy, bless her heart, tried to help with that, but she kept involuntarily adding the "a double-s" word every time she had to call the pig Jack.

Since that didn't work out well, it was up to me alone to keep an eye on the pig's rehearsal schedule.

We worked hard, too. Because even though I thought casting day would be a romp in the park for him, Cunningham didn't want people thinking he acquired the role by being the playwright's pet. I hear that happens a lot in Hollywood.

So, Cunningham—aka Jack—practiced his dog skills repeatedly. The pig quickly learned how to roll over, fetch a corncob and play dead. But, since he didn't speak fluent dog, we spent hours working on that with a local beagle named Cooper acting as his tutor.

Pretty soon, even the neighbors couldn't tell Cooper from Cunningham, especially at night.

Once we got the language thing down pat, Cunningham—aka Jack—started chasing cars to perfect his character. He got so good at doing that, one of the other neighbors even mentioned it to the Sheriff.

By casting day, Cunningham—aka Jack—was not only off-book, but he was smoking like the hot dog actor he is.

So, as a treat, I let him roll down the truck's passenger door window on the way over to the college. That way, he could stick his head out and practice panting, too.

We didn't know this until later, but as a practical joke, my wife had called ahead to the theatre department and told whoever answered the phone there that a mad man with a rabid pig was headed their way.

The woman's sense of humor is priceless.

As a result, when we pulled up to the theater, the play's director and several campus security members, who—we later learned—didn't understand Judy's wit at all, were standing by to greet us.

I thought that was strange. But, then again, I *was* the playwright, and Cunningham a well-known star.

The greeting party, for some reason, even included the head of the psychology department.

Cunningham—aka Jack—wagged his tail and smiled real loud at them. Then he barked a friendly hello.

Even so, the group seemed nervous, which, at first, made me think we might have come on the wrong day.

"The pig is here to try out for the play," I said. "He wants to be the dog. I'm the one who wrote it. But I guess you know that."

The psychology department head stepped forward and said, rather rudely, "This is a pig-free campus. It has been for years."

"But," I said. "Cunningham—aka Jack—just wants to try out for the role of the dog. Did I mention I have an Agricultural Journalism Degree from the University of Georgia?"

That typically carries more weight than it did with this bunch.

"I don't care," he said, and I think he meant it. "The only role that pig can play here is in the dining hall."

That seemed strange. But maybe they were overcrowded or something. Who knows?

What happened next is sort of a blur.

When one of the security guard ladies inadvertently put her hand on her nightstick, Cunningham—aka Jack—mistook it for another one of those electric cattle prods. So, he, quite naturally, panicked and jumped out the truck window.

Then he headed for the hills of Habersham, barking like a dog in church.

I think that tender loin he had because of a pulled hamstring is the only thing that kept him from running all the way to Clarkesville.

After I caught up, we heard on the radio that some hound from Young Harris had just nailed the dog part.

The very next week, that dog's picture was on the front page of *Society News* magazine.

Stupid dog.

My pig was so upset, he howled all the way home.

I've got those
new truck radio blues

My pet pig, Cunningham, and I recently went shopping for a newer model pickup truck.

The transmission finally dropped out of my old one—his name was Scrap Iron—over on Highway 129.

We never did find it.

I do like the new truck, although my wife, Judy, hates the color. As she's pointed out several times now, it was probably a mistake to let Cunningham pick that out. That's because, colorblind or not, a pig will go for corn yellow nine times out of ten.

But I'd already promised him he could, so my hands were tied.

The only real issue I have with the new truck—Judy's already nicknamed him Gus the Guzzler—is the radio.

Now, I've never been at the top of my class. But then again, I've never been at the bottom of it either, except for math.

But I don't think even Al Einstein could operate the radio in this new truck.

Ole Scrap Iron had a much simpler radio. You turned the knob—it came on. When you turned that knob the other way, it went off. A second knob made changing channels a piece of cake, too.

It was a thing of simplistic beauty.

Even Cunningham could handle that old radio, although changing channels sometimes made his snout sore, especially on dirt roads.

My new truck's radio doesn't have any knobs at all. I guess that should have been a red flag, but the salesman assured me I would soon "take to" going knobless.

Well, bless his little technology-unchallenged heart, he was wrong.

The only thing I want to "take to" that radio is a hammer. I won't even say what Cunningham would like to do to it. He's not been able to pick up WPIG out of Des Moines since we got the darn thing.

He's pretty fed up, even for a pig.

After weeks of trying to get the radio to act right, I decided to ask for help from the smartest man I know—my neighbor Chuck.

Chuck's a retired pilot who, rumor has it, once made an emergency landing on Mark Zuckerberg's yacht. That and a few other incidents earned him his nickname of Chuck Jägermeister.

Before too long, ole Chuck came over and climbed into the passenger seat.

"I see you have Bluetooth," he said, which I found hurtful. I started to tell him he had bad breath but held my tongue.

"What's the problem with the radio?" Chuck asked, giving Cunningham, who had hopped up on the seat to supervise, the cold shoulder. That man's been cross with my pig ever since the little fellow started taking naps on his porch last summer.

"I can't turn it on. There's no knob. I think it's defective."

"First of all, it's not a radio," said Chuck. "It's an infotainment unit."

"Whatever," I said. "I'd just want the darn thing set so I can listen to the Swap Shop on WRWH in Cleveland. The Georgia Cleveland. Not the one in Tennessee. WPIG in Des Moines, too, if you can manage it."

"You have to touch that little house there first," Chuck said, pointing to a picture on the panel.

Who would have thought?

When I did, the screen lit up like I'd hit the jackpot on a slot machine at Six Flags. Cunningham panicked, scrambled over Chuck's legs, and ran to his safe place under the man's porch.

I panicked a little, too, but Chuck pulled me back inside. "It's important not to be afraid of your infotainment unit," he said. "You just have to show it who's boss. Now, choose the choice you want and touch the corresponding icon. You can do this."

Not knowing what an icon was, I looked the screen over. Of the dozen or so options offered, the only ones that made any sense at all were named Settings and My Music.

"I'll take 'Settings' for $400," I said to Chuck, hoping not to jeopardize the situation.

Chuck wasn't amused. "Do you want my help or not?"

"Yes, please."

"Okay. Touch 'Source' then."

When I did, another amusingly colored screen popped up. This one offered several more possibilities to be touched. Doing all this touchy-feely stuff to a radio seemed unnecessary—not to mention unsanitary. But maybe that's just me.

I could see Chuck was stressing some, so I reached over to tap one of the pictures on the screen, thinking I'd at least be showing initiative. However, I inadvertently touched an image of a little green apple instead.

Well, you would have thought I'd slapped Chuck's mama. "You hit the wrong one!" he said, using his pilot voice. "On an airplane, you would have just dumped both fuel tanks."

"Sorry," I said. This time, hoping to make Chuck happy, I touched My Music.

"Is that what you want? To hear your music?" Chuck asked.

"No. I can't even play the piano. And even if I could, how on earth would the radio know about it?"

All this was getting to be just a little bit too Big Brother for my taste.

Chuck shook his head. "I'm talking about the music on your iPhone."

"What's an eye phone?"

At this point, Chuck got out and walked over to his house. I thought he might be going for a tool or something, but he never came back.

It's been a month now, and I still haven't been able to listen to the Swap Shop.

Plus, every time Cunningham touches the radio, some British lady named Sara starts insisting we make a U-turn immediately.

I'd give anything to have my old knobs back.

Why hogs hate hurricanes

I think the unnatural fear pigs feel for hurricanes—wind of any kind, really—goes back to that story about a grey wolf, wearing, as I recall, a little red riding hood and allegedly blowing down several houses.

I've explained over and over that today's building codes are much stricter, but I think the damage is already done.

And, when Cunningham heard a hurricane named Irma was headed our way, he got even more nervous than usual.

You see, Irma is Cunningham's mama's name. And nobody wants to hear that they've named a hurricane after their mama, I don't care who you are.

He's way too well-bred to mention this, but Miss Irma was a Yorkshire out of Oxford. His daddy, Tamworth, is descended from a long line of English Berkshires.

That's not really part of this story, but I thought you might like to know.

I tried to keep the news of Hurricane Irma's impending approach from Cunningham as long as possible. But if you'll recall, warnings for that storm were the only thing on television for nearly two months.

Also, the weather folks couldn't make up their minds about where they expected Irma to land. In their defense, it's hard to predict where the first frost will hit, let alone a hurricane.

Cunningham was enjoying a rerun of that timeless TV classic, *Green Acres*, on the RFD-TV channel when he heard the news. A *Farm News Alert* reporter interrupted the show to talk about Irma.

At first, Cunningham thought his mama had won another blue ribbon at the fair. But after they showed several weather people standing knee-deep in the breakers, he quickly figured out what was going on.

On that particular day, current computer cones showed Irma would land somewhere in Northeast Iowa. Since Cunningham still has lots of family up that way, including his mama, this news caused him concern.

Two weeks later, even more current computer cones shifted Irma's likely landfall to Western Canada, and Cunningham breathed a brief sigh of relief.

But, by the next week, the TV weather people had changed their minds again.

This time they were thinking Irma would hit Myrtle Beach and then head on over our way.

By now, Cunningham was a wreck. I think everybody was, really.

Expecting the power to go off, Cunningham filled his water bucket, stockpiled acorns and even rooted up a few bricks to pile around his pigsty.

While people head to the liqu… I mean grocery store before a big storm hits, pigs look to their local pig food store for provisions.

So, I loaded Cunningham in the truck and headed for the local liqu… I mean The Old Sautee Tea Room and Pig Food Store. The plan was to stock up on peppermint pig pellets.

The wind had already picked up when we got there, so I told Cunningham to stay in the truck while I went inside to place his order.

"I'd like thirty-four bags of peppermint pig pellets," I said politely to that loading dock director, who raises colorful chickens for a hobby.

"Sorry. We're all out," he replied.

"How can you be out of peppermint pig pellets?" I asked. "Y'all buy the darn things by the truckload."

"There's been a run. Because of the hurricane, I guess."

"But I saw peppermint pig pellets in the warehouse when we drove up," I pointed out.

"No, you didn't."

"Yes, I did."

"Well, even if you did, your account is way past due."

"You're never going to let me forget that are you?"

I was about to inform him that we'd been thrown out of nicer places than this, when we overheard what sounded like a truck crashing through a tin-sided warehouse wall. I'd heard that sound before during the war—I forget which one—so I knew it well.

I was stationed in Albuquerque and on KP duty at the time, but still, once you hear the sound of a truck crashing through a tin-sided warehouse wall—well, let's just say you never forget it.

As I explained to the deputy later, after Cunningham dozed off on the truck seat, he started having that dream he gets where he's saving Judy Garland's little dog in the *Wizard of Oz*.

He has that same dream every time the wind gets up.

Now, when Cunningham dreams, his upside hind leg rotates in a series of counterclockwise motions. Since I have an Agricultural Journalism Degree from the University of Georgia, I can confidently tell you that's called restless ham syndrome.

There's no cure for it.

His hoof accidentally shifted the darn thing into neutral. I hadn't set the parking brake because I don't want that one to wear out too soon the way the one on my old truck did.

Gravity, as it always does, came into play and pulled the truck downhill. The rapid burst of speed caused the vehicle to sideswipe the loading dock director's car, remove the side-mirror from a customer's truck and ultimately crash into the tin-sided warehouse.

Looking back on it, using my one phone call to remind Animal Control to give Cunningham an extra blanket may have been a mistake.

I probably should have called my wife for bail money instead.

Cunningham used his to call his mama, Irma.

On the plus side, the pig and I both got to ride out that storm in a safe, county-maintained building equipped with a tin roof and generators.

My wife wanted to bring bail money, but unfortunately, she couldn't get the car out for about two weeks.

Due to all the rain, I guess.

Mr. Pig goes to Washington

My pet pig, Cunningham, is extremely patriotic. For a pig, I mean.

And so, as you can imagine, he's always dreamed of visiting our nation's capital. Since I had dreamed about that once myself, we decided to drive on up there and look around.

My wife, Judy, went to Washington on her high school senior trip, so she decided to stay home this time. After all, how much could the place have changed in forty years?

Once the pig and I arrived in DC—that's what the locals call it—I looked at a list of hotels and tapped one called Watergate. I felt like Cunningham might relax better there, since he loves water and is comfortable with gates.

Besides, it seemed like I'd heard good things about that hotel sometime back.

In spite of its name, it turns out the Watergate Hotel isn't all that pig friendly. Neither were any of the other places we tried, including one with a red roof, which Cunningham liked because it reminded him of a barn.

So, in the end, we decided to camp in that little park across the street from the large white house they keep up for the presidents to live in. That way, we'd be all set to be first in line for the morning tour.

Cunningham was so excited he started chasing his tail.

We had no sooner unloaded the truck and pitched our tent than a crowd began to gather. It seemed like people came from everywhere. They were carrying signs, jumping up and down and hollering to beat the band. Some of them even had loudspeakers.

I figured the president must be coming in from a trip or something, and they were all here to say hello.

One of the ladies holding a sign walked over to us and looked at Cunningham.

"COOL," she shouted at me over the noise.

"YES. I AM GLAD IT'S NOT TOO HOT. PIGS DON'T HAVE MANY SWEAT GLANDS, YOU KNOW," I shouted back.

"NO. I MEAN BRINGING A REAL PIG TO WASHINGTON TO SYMBOLIZE THE OPPRESSION OF THE WORKING CLASS."

"OH. WELL, I ACTUALLY JUST BROUGHT HIM TO SEE THE CAPITAL."

"WE'RE NOT PROTESTING THERE UNTIL TOMORROW," she yelled back. "COME JOIN US!"

"WELL, I'M NOT REALLY THE TYPE TO MAKE A FUSS."

Since I was almost hoarse from speaking in upper case so long, Cunningham and I decided we might ought to ease on back toward the truck. We both hated to miss seeing the president's chopper land, but things were way too loud around there already.

Plus, I was fairly sure a few of these people had been drinking.

We decided to visit the National Mall next. But if there was a store there, we sure couldn't find it.

After that, Cunningham and I went to the Capitol building, which looked nice, even from a distance. I mean, with that big dome and all. But have you seen those steps out front? No wonder those Senators are in such good shape.

Cunningham and I both decided to pass on going inside.

By this time, we were getting pretty hungry. So, we found a restaurant and looked at the menu somebody had framed and hung outside by the door. I guess the head waiter must have noticed we were interested in eating there because he quickly came outside.

"May I help you?" he asked, rather snootily, I thought. I did admire his suit, though. It made me wonder how many pairs of socks a man like that might own.

From the way that man looked at Cunningham, I decided I'd better make sure he knew the pig and I were together.

"Do you serve pigs here?"

"Of course, we do," he replied. "But please take him around back. Our chef does the procuring."

We decided to pass on his offer.

Instead, we walked over to another one of those numerous little grassy spots they have up there to eat a handful of the boiled peanuts we'd brought with us. I almost forgot about having them.

Just as we sat down, a well-known congressman walked up. I could tell he was a well-known congressman because of how he introduced himself.

"Hello," he said, nearly shaking my hand off. "I'm a well-known congressman. Welcome to DC. That's a mighty fine-looking pig you got there. Would you like to buy the Washington Monument?"

"I didn't know it was for sale," I said, not wanting to appear too interested right off the bat.

He went on to clarify that his committee had just voted to shut down several monuments to save the country some money. He explained that due to the cost-savings on electricity alone, they could let this one go for a song to the right deserving citizen.

As luck would have it, he—being the committee chairman—even had the deed with him. When he told me the asking price, I didn't see how I could pass it up. Those little windows at the top had to be worth at least that much.

So, I got out Judy's checkbook and started making the check to, as the congressman suggested, the Committee Advertising Sanctified Headstones—C.A.S.H. for short.

I was just about to sign it when a policeman walked up. I guess the congressman must have been paged or something because he ran off in a hurry without even taking my check.

The policeman was nice enough to hang around, though.

Then he asked, "Where were you between five and six?"

"In pre-school," I replied, honestly.

"Listen. I know what you're up to. You're using that pig to symbolize the oppression of the working class. Didn't I just see you two in front of the White House a while ago?"

"Yes. But we didn't go in. I don't even think the President was home."

The policeman reached out his hand and said, "Papers."

I immediately answered, "Scissors. I win!"

I guess the police in DC don't have much of a sense of humor because he didn't laugh. And that was pretty funny, I don't care who you are.

Instead, he blew his whistle real loud, which scared Cunningham bad.

By the time I caught up with him, the pig was all the way back at the truck.

With so many sirens going off at the same time, we figured it might be best to just head on back home, so we did.

My only regret is that Cunningham didn't get to see the Bay of Pigs Memorial.

He would have enjoyed that.

How I met Cunningham

During the recent "flu-like" season, several of you (okay, it was just the one guy) sent a number of cards and letters asking how my pet pig, Cunningham, was coping.

That man also asked how I met Cunningham in the first place.

Since other people might also be interested in the answers to those questions, I will try my best to resolve both issues in the space available here.

First of all, Cunningham held up nicely; thank you for asking. However, any time the flu shows up, he always insists on calling it a pigdemic. Pigs, bless their hearts, can sometimes be prone to hyporkondria.

This staying-at-home-with-a-hog thing was rough on my wife, Judy. In her defense, being in the house with a pig all day is harder than most people think it is. Particularly when it gets too cold to open the windows.

It was especially tough back when we only had the one television.

While you do tend to wash your hands more when there's a hog in the house, not touching your face, as the medical people on television recommend, is still tricky.

However, Judy picked up a helpful tidbit on the innerweb that really helped her with that face-touching thing—she just kept a glass of wine in each hand.

Despite the cold weather, Cunningham and I tried to assist her all winter by cooking ribs and such outside as much as possible on my Little Blue Egg.

That gave Judy a break. You see, after she got the salad made, prepared the vegetables, made dessert, and had the ribs ready to go, I put the meat on the grill.

That kept her from having to do any heavy lifting. Then, once she got the plates and silverware on the table and made sweet tea, we ate.

After dinner, all Judy had to do was the dishes.

Between Cunningham's love of peppermint pig pellets, and my appreciation for pie and barbecue, the pig and I both put on a few extra pounds over the winter. Truth is, he became quite a porker. And pigs just can't carry those extra pounds as well as people do.

As a result, his pigiatrician at the hog hospital in Homer has him on a strict diet of sweet potatoes, parsnips and water until he drops a hundred pounds or so.

My wife hinted I should go on a diet, too. Her first hint was a note on the refrigerator door saying, "This is not your happy place."

She's always wanted me, bless her heart, to get down to the weight they put on my driver's license, but that hasn't been right since high school. I keep reminding her I have a condition that prevents me from dieting.

It's called hunger.

Anyway, the doctor says my weight is fine. I just need to work on my height a little bit.

But I digress. I personally enjoyed staying home with Cunningham over those winter months.

In fact, it got me thinking about old times, which brings me to that guy's second question—how Cunningham and I met in the first place.

A few years back, when our TV was on the blink, I drove my pickup to Atlanta to see a Braves game up close and personal.

I was taking that shortcut past the livestock auction barn on Market Street, trying unsuccessfully to avoid I-285 when, much to my amazement, I noticed a little pig hitchhiking by the side of the road.

I guess I shouldn't have been surprised. I mean, I *was* on Market Street.

No sooner had I picked the little fella up than a Cobb County deputy pulled up behind me and indicated he'd like to chat for a second.

"What are you doing with that pig?" he asked.

"Nothing illegal," I reassured the officer. "I'm just giving him a ride. He was hitchhiking, you see. Nobody else would pick him up."

The deputy said, "We have laws down here. If you don't take that pig to the zoo or someplace similar right now, I'm going to give you a ticket."

He didn't say to what.

Still, not wanting any trouble with the law, I made a quick detour to the zoo. The pig and I had such a good time there, I decided to take him to the ballgame, too.

We were just coming out of the Chop House when little Cunningham inadvertently caught a fly ball in his mouth.

He got so excited when they flashed his picture up on the big screen, he swallowed the darn thing whole. Then, probably thinking he was going to have to replace or pay for it, Cunningham panicked.

He struck out for the field, cleared the bases and slid home like a pro, which was good. Because they could have just as easily called that a foul ball.

As far as I know, that still holds the record for being the Braves' first "inside the pork" home run.

Cunningham even got his picture taken with Bobby Cox, although Bobby didn't smile like he usually does when something like that happens.

Since Cunningham didn't have any post-game plans, I brought him home with me, and the rest is history.

Judy wasn't quite as pleased about my new pet pig as I'd hoped she'd be, though.

I guess she was hoping for another kitten, bless her heart.

A pig with one eye

I may have mentioned that my cousin, Wayne, has a pet pig of his own named Jerry Lee.

However, I may not have mentioned that Jerry Lee was, sadly, born with a birth defect—he only has one eye.

They think it may have been because his mama stayed too long under one of those solar heat lamps they use in that part of Illinois where Jerry Lee's family is from. It was her first litter, and she just didn't know any better.

Even with only one eye, Jerry Lee sees fine. Why, with that big ole eye right in the middle of his forehead, he can probably spot things quicker than the rest of us.

Back when Wayne first laid eyes on Jerry Lee at the pet pig adoption center in Adel, it was love at first sight.

Because of his unfortunate flaw, the little fella had been passed over by a lot of potential pig owners who couldn't see past that one big eye. But not Wayne.

As soon as the two of them made three-way eye contact, it was love at first sight.

Jerry Lee has never let being a one-eyed pig hold him back. In fact, he can usually beat Cunningham at horseshoes, and every so often, at checkers. Although I think Cunningham sometimes lets Jerry Lee win on purpose, bless his heart.

A while back, Wayne got to studying about Jerry Lee and wondering if anything could be done for his pig's eye. His girlfriend, Viola Mae, suggested they take him down to the University of Georgia's veterinarian school and see what they thought about it.

So, the two of them loaded up the pig and headed for Athens. Now, Wayne, not having an Agricultural Journalism Degree from the University of Georgia like I do, wasn't all that familiar with the campus.

Neither was Viola Mae, although she did know how to get to The Varsity.

No sooner had they downed their chili dogs and pulled out of the parking lot, than Wayne, Jerry Lee and Viola Mae got lost.

Then, somehow or other, they made a wrong turn at the student center and drove out onto the football field. They didn't see the famous bulldog, ole Uga, anywhere. But one of the assistant coaches had most of the other Georgia players out there rehearsing for next week's game.

According to Wayne, the man was pretty mad about him being on the grass with the truck. I guess there had been a big rain the night before.

While Wayne explained that he was trying to find the vet school—specifically the hog department—the coach looked in and saw Jerry Lee.

"What on earth is wrong with that hog?" he asked.

"Not much," said Wayne. "He just has one eye, though."

The coach hollered for the team to sprint on over to the truck.

"Hey, boys," he shouted. "Come over here and look at this pig with one eye!"

And they did.

And that's when Jerry Lee became a die-hard Bulldog fan.

Let's root out hog fighting once and for all

My cousin, Wayne, once wallowed in the filthy pastime of hog fighting.

In fact, Wayne even became the Hog-Fighting Champion of the World, and—although he won't wear it in public—he has the belt buckle to prove it.

Sadly, having your cousin become a hog-fighting champion is one of those things that makes a family proud and mortified at the same time.

It's like when your sister wins the tobacco-spitting contest at the county fair—which Wayne's sister has, by the way, three times.

Wayne's retired from all that muddle now, but the burden of having been involved in hog fighting at all weighs on him like an unopened bag of feed corn.

When he heard I was writing a book about pigs, Wayne asked if he might have a little space in it to unburden himself by telling his story.

I had to charge him, of course, but I didn't have the heart to say no. I mean, he *is* my cousin.

So, below, in his own words, although thankfully not his own handwriting, is Wayne's story.

Go for it, buddy. But you still owe me ten bucks for this, remember?

Confessions of a hog-fighter

by Cousin Wayne

Hello. My name is Wayne.

I'm a recovering hog-fighter.

There I've said it, and it feels good. I don't fight hogs n'more. But for those of you considering this so-called sport—either as a participant, spectator, or both—you need to hear my story.

But I warn you. It's sloppy.

I know now I should have just walked away the first time some pig called a runt (they pronounce it "grunt"), but I didn't. Instead, I tried to smoke that porker, but he penned me quicker than Jimmy Dean could say sausage.

Determined not to be just another piece of white meat, or to ever let another boar bust my chops,

I put my Harley in hock and went to the gym. Twice.

Before long, I didn't just enjoy hog fighting; I was good at it. Once I learned karate, I became well-known for my signature move—something I called the pork chop.

Later, I joined a farm team in the Tenderloin League. But after winning the Sizzling Medallion three years running, I jumped the fence to the Larder Class. That's as big as it gets in the pig leagues.

Often, it was offal. Some of those porkers were as clumsy as a hog on ice. But it was almost like other pigs could take flight.

I don't know how widespread hog fighting is today, but I've heard there are feeder operations all over the country, particularly in the corn belt.

I told myself I could quit anytime, but that was hogwash. I was addicted to penning pigs. It was like I had swine fever.

Trying to quit was as useless as well... you know.

Hog fighting soon showed its ugly underbelly when gamblers begin emerging like the swine they are.

I never understood how they knew when a hog fight was about to break out, but they had their links—it was almost like they could smell it.

I can still see the faces of the men in the crowd with their "GO HOGS" caps, and those women with those silk purses slung over their shoulders.

I could name names, but I'm no squealer.

When I was on top, they called me The Butcher. Later, after I developed a pork belly and jowls, they cruelly nicknamed me The Chubby Chitlin.

Hog fighting ground me up until, finally, it rendered me useless.

The low point was the night I got my butt kicked in Boston.

Stopping this menace will be tough because, believe it or not, hog fighting is legal in every state except Texas.

That's right; there's no national law against picking a fight with a pig. And don't expect much help from Washington, with their pork-barrel politics and all that other tripe.

It's too late for me. But if exposing my tale can keep one person from wallowing in the crackling pit of hog fighting, then coming clean will be worth every bacon bit.

In closing, I'd just like to say—don't do this, boys and girls. You'll only wind up bacon your mama's heart.

Any farmer will tell you pigs talk a lot. In fact, they have at least 20 different vocalizations. And when a pig squeals, it can be as loud as 115 decibels. That's near the level of a jet engine on take-off, which explains why so many pig farmers are hard of hearing.

About Cunningham

I guess you could say that Cunningham was born the same day he kicked the bucket.

That may sound paradoxical, so, let me explain.

You see, one Saturday morning, I was reading our local newspaper while my wife, Judy, and I sipped our morning coffee on the porch.

Keep in mind that one of the most widely read parts of any decent small-town weekly is something often called *The Blotter*. Whatever they call it, that's where the editor puts the local arrest records, traffic stops, and such.

In other words, it's the most popular part of the paper.

The third item from the top that week was one sentence stating police had responded to a request from someone wanting to have a deceased pig removed from their driveway.

Always alert for a good column idea, that struck me as a no-brainer. After all, most people go their whole lives without having to have a dead pig taken away before they can back the car out—once you get out of Iowa, anyhow.

So, I folded the paper, polished off my coffee and headed for my office.

"Where are you going?" asked Judy.

"To write a column about a pig."

"Sounds nice," she said, pouring herself another cup. Then she yawned. "Have fun."

"I will," I said. And I did.

The next day, I sent the following words to the newspaper.

A sorry blot on an otherwise perfect pig

A recent edition of this newspaper indicated that someone had inadvertently left a deceased pig that had died of suspected natural causes on a driveway in the Town Creek community.

I'm afraid it may have been me.

You see, last week, I took my pet pig, Cunningham, to the hog hospital in Homer to get his annual swine flu shot. As a special treat, I let him ride home in the back of the truck instead of up front on the seat with me—something I now know was a mistake.

I noticed Cunningham wasn't still in the truck when I got home, but to tell the truth, I figured he'd jumped off at the red light to sneak up to the Farmer's Exchange.

I'd told him we didn't have time to stop there that day, and he was all sulled up about it.

In my defense, I was in a hurry to get to the house to check my cell phone messages.

I planned to let Cunningham watch a full hour of *Mud Wrestling Mania* to make up for it but decided to wait till we got home to tell him. Now he'll never know.

I write all this to explain why I didn't report him missing. You see, we've never had him neutered, and Cunningham is bad to sneak off.

He knows his way home, so I wasn't really worried.

But I guess he must have gotten confused about the new right turn south of Cleveland and taken the Appalachian Parkway by mistake.

I've done that myself. I think we all have.

Nothing confuses a pig like a parkway, but if he had only looked up, he could have seen Yonah Mountain and that big, three-story pigpen I built for him up here. My wife calls it the sty-scraper.

Instead, he turned left, then took the right fork and wound up in trouble on Town Creek Road—something else I've done myself.

I can only imagine Cunningham's final hours. I know he would have tried to flag down a ride, but people don't pick up hitchhiking pigs the way they used to. I blame *The Muppet Show* for that.

I suppose he just walked until his little pig's feet gave out.

It's easy to jump to conclusions when you hear about a dead pig showing up in somebody's driveway. And since Cunningham already has five brothers in the pen, I suppose it's inevitable that some will think the worst.

But that's hogwash; Cunningham was a fine swine, I tell you what.

He wasn't perfect. No pig is. In fact, just last week, Judy caught Cunningham eating a dictionary. No damage was done, though—she took the words right out of his mouth.

The paper didn't say who found Cunningham, but I hope whoever did treated his remains with respect.

My one regret is that he wasn't wrapped in his favorite blanket.

I guess it's too much to wish for, but I hope—before they buried him—somebody thought to put a little pig's tie around his neck.

Cunningham would have liked that.

* * * *

After the column ran, I figured that was that. However, a few days later, I got a call from the editor.

"Hello," I said.

"This is Billy Chism. The editor. For some reason I don't fully understand, we had a good response to your pig column. Especially in that elusive women-over-forty demographic. You need to write something else about him."

"I can't," I said back. "The pig's dead, remember? You reported it in *The Blotter*."

"Well," said Billy. "Bring him back to life."

So, the following week, I had Cunningham come home. *The Blotter* pig wasn't about him. It was all a colossal mistake.

Billy's successor, Wayne Hardy, took a liking to Cunningham, too. In fact, I'm thinking of letting Cunningham spend every other weekend at his house next year. So, many thanks to Wayne—the editor, not my cousin.

All in all, that pig and I have walked down, up, and around many happy trails together. And, hopefully, we've made a few people smile, forget their troubles for a bit, and maybe even laugh a little.

Indeed, Cunningham is alive and well.

In fact, he just came in with a little leaflet about the Appalachian Trail, although I don't think they allow pigs on that one.

However, it doesn't mention that in the brochure.

Is a pet pig right for you?

Many people have questions about whether or not a pet pig is right for them. And, drawing on my Agricultural Journalism Degree from the University of Georgia, I'll answer a few of the most common queries right here.

It's the least I can do. I mean, with you buying this book, and all.

There are several things you'll want to consider before bringing a hog home.

Especially if you're married.

So, I've compiled a few of the most common questions Cunningham and I have gotten over the years about pig ownership.

You can thank me later.

- ❖ Q: *Can I keep a pet pig in my apartment?*
- ❖ A: I doubt it. I mean, it's okay with me if it's okay with the pig and your landlord. Just be aware that you might not get your deposit back.

❖ Q: *Can pigs bite?*

❖ A: Absolutely. In fact, a large hog can devour a small human in under eight minutes. That's why it's essential to teach your pig good manners early on.

❖ Q: *Can I play catch with my pig?*

❖ A: Probably. I'd stay away from footballs, though because of that pigskin issue.

❖ Q: *Can I teach a pig to fetch my slippers?*

❖ A: In theory. Although you may not want to wear what's left of them after they do.

❖ Q: *Are pigs affectionate?*

❖ A: Yes. And sometimes at the most inappropriate times.

❖ Q: *How do I "pig proof" my house?*

❖ A: You know, that's a really good question. I wish I knew. However, most good farm supply stores do carry piglet outlet covers.

❖ Q: *Can a pig be housebroken?*

❖ A: Absolutely. My pet pig, Cunningham, has broken tons of things in our house. You'll have to ask my wife for the complete list, but believe me, she knows it by heart.

❖ Q: *Can I take my pet pig on vacation?*

❖ A: Yes. Although, many airlines are reluctant to sell tickets to pigs. Especially in first class, which is the only place a good-size hog can really be comfortable.

- ❖ Q: *Do my pig's toenails need to be trimmed?*
- ❖ A: They do. But be careful. And NEVER take the pig to the same place where your wife has hers done. Trust me.

I think that about covers everything. If you have additional questions, it might be better if you talked to my wife directly.

The End

No, wait!

I almost forgot. I have one more pig story for you.

While we were debating hogs the other day, my friend, a great columnist and author to boot, Phil Hudgins, mentioned that he also had a pretty good swine story to tell. So, here, and at no extra charge to you, I might add, is Phil's pig story.

Think of it as a bonus. Although, since Phil wouldn't agree to pay for it, I couldn't afford to have an illustration drawn for this one.

Want a pet to love you unconditionally? Find an unattractive pig

by Phil Hudgins

While doing some heavy reading the other day, I came across a story about pigs using tools.

The fellow who wrote this book probably wouldn't have been surprised about that, but the researchers were.

They already knew that chimps and dolphins make use of tools, but not pigs. But then, an ecologist watched as a wild pig in a Parisian zoo picked up a piece of bark with its mouth and dug in the dirt with it.

Mrs. Piggy was building a nest, something she does every six months to get ready for another litter of piglets.

Three other pigs in the pen did the same thing.

Lucy built nests too, but she used pillows. She was a pot-bellied pig who belonged to the Hart family—Joe, Cindy, Kristi and Kathi.

Lucy was a house pet, along with Major the dog, and Snuggles and Lacy the cats.

This little pig thought she was a dog, too—she loved to bark—but her pig instincts took over at nesting time, which came about every two weeks. Lucy may have been a little confused, but she knew enough to push sofa pillows into a pile, just in case.

She didn't know she'd been spayed.

"Lucy was not a pretty pig," said Kathi. In human terms, you would describe her as having a deviated septum with nosebleeds. And she sneezed a lot—not a good combination.

But she was gentle and loving, unlike Walter, her handsome porcine predecessor, who used his tusks as tools to eat sheetrock and ended up being sent back to the farm to cavort with Elvis, a pig who thought he was a horse.

The Hart family lived on Georgia's Lake Oconee during this era, and Lucy was happy as a pig in sunshine. Which is where she often stayed, along with Major the golden retriever, sleeping on the lake's shore.

At day's end, the girls bathed Lucy and rubbed her down with baby oil. Then she was ready to sit in her friends' laps, munch on pork rinds and watch TV.

One downside to being a pampered pig was getting shots to control her nosebleeds. Inoculating a 100-pound pig was not easy, the Harts agreed. They must have stuck her when her back was turned.

Otherwise, Lucy had it made. This potty-trained porker ate three times a day, went for walks on a leash, and relaxed wherever she was.

She got into serious trouble once when she ate some homework belonging to one of the girls. The teacher didn't believe a pig would eat homework. A dog maybe, but not a pig.

Cindy took Lucy to school to prove the culprit was a pig.

Lucy got a fishhook caught in her mouth only one time, and she seldom bit into electrical cords. She loved drinking sugar water from the base of the Christmas tree, but that was no big deal.

When the Harts moved to a close neighborhood in the city, they had to find a new home for Lucy. It was a sad time. Things weren't the same without her.

Everybody loved Lucy.

"That's all folks!"

About the Author

Emory Jones grew up on a farm in White County, Georgia. After a stint in the Air Force, he joined Gold Kist Inc. as publications manager. He has been the Southeastern editor for *Farm Journal Magazine* and executive vice president at Freebairn & Company, an Atlanta-based advertising agency where he managed the firm's agricultural accounts.

During his career, Emory interviewed and photographed farmers in all fifty states and had articles published in numerous US farm publications.

He has written seven other books, including: *White County 101*; *Distant Voices—The Story of the Nacoochee Valley Indian Mound*; *Heart of a Co-op—The HEMC Story*; *Zipping Through Georgia on a Goat-Powered Time Machine*; *Helen 101*; and *Memories Etched in Pott'ry*, a creative memoir set in his Great Uncle Cheever Meaders' pottery shop in 1958.

Emory's first novel, *The Valley Where They Danced*, takes place in the Northeast Georgia mountains just after WWI.

Two of his books, *The Valley Where They Danced* and *Memories Etched in Pott'ry*, have been made into plays and performed in Northeast Georgia theaters. Two other plays are in the works.

Emory sits on the board of the White County Historical Society and is an avid folk pottery collector. He and his wife, Judy, and cat, Rowdy Yates, live on Yonah Mountain in White County, Georgia.

And—I almost forgot—he has an Agricultural Journalism Degree from the University of Georgia.

About the Illustrator

 While Jim never earned an Agricultural Journalism Degree, he did grow up on his multi-generation family farm and spent half his working career as a small-town newspaper editor.

His grandfather had a small country store in the yard of their home where neighbors dropped by for a jug of milk, a plug of tobacco and lots of talk. Between the RC colas and Moon Pies, Jim absorbed discussions of religion, politics, hound dogs, weather, pocketknife swaps and taxes. All this was early training for his editorial cartoons business.

Jim served as a State Officer in the FFA in high school and earned two degrees from Young Harris College and a degree in English from Piedmont College.

When pitching his editorial cartoons to the *North Georgia News*, he was offered a job and became editor of the *Towns County Herald* for the next fifteen years. He began syndicating his editorial cartoons, and today, numerous papers in Georgia and North Carolina carry Powell Cartoons.

Jim has spent twenty years in telecommunications. He has managed a cablecast TV station in North Georgia, and currently serves as a product manager in Windstream's marketing department.

Jim and his wife, Roxanne, and their dog, Charlie, enjoy the quiet beauty of life in the southern Appalachians on his family's farm in Young Harris. They are committed Christians and members of the House of Prayer Interdenominational Church in Blairsville.